LATINAS

Other books from Red Sugarcane Press, Inc.

A Mirror in My Own Backstage
Poetry and prose by José Angel Figueroa

Growing Up Gonzales
A Play by Felix Rojas

Julia de Burgos: Child of Water
A Play by Carmen Rivera

Shameless Woman
Poetry and prose by Magdalena Gómez

Through the Eyes of Rebel Women:
The Young Lords, 1969-1976
A herstory by Iris Morales

Un Espejo En Mi Proprio Bastidor
Poetry and prose by José Angel Figueroa

LATINAS

Struggles & Protests in 21st Century USA

Edited by

Iris Morales

Red Sugarcane Press, Inc.
New York, New York

Latinas: Struggles & Protests in 21st Century USA
Copyright © 2018 by Iris Morales

Published by Red Sugarcane Press, Inc.
534 West 112th Street, #250404
New York, NY 10025
www.redsugarcanepress.com
info@redsugarcanepress.com

Cover Artwork: Mia Roman
Layout Design: Iris Morales

ISBN: 13: 978-0-9968276-4-5
E-book: 13: 978-0-9968276-5-2
Library of Congress Control Number: 2017961956

First Edition
Printed in the United States of America

I dedicate this book to the memory of
my sister Minerva Morales who understood the
relation between healing and transformation,
and believed in rebirth.

CONTENTS

FOREWORD

DEBORAH PAREDEZ, PH.D.

The first time I met Iris Morales was on a Sunday afternoon in Harlem just before the first disastrous election of the 21st century. It was less than a handful of years after the release of Iris's monumental documentary, *¡Palante, Siempre Palante!*, which I was planning to teach in my seminar about Latina/o arts and culture. I was just beginning my career as a professor, just beginning in many ways to understand myself in relation to the tradition of Latina activists, artists, and thinkers who had paved the way for my arrival. That afternoon and in the many since then, I stood awe-struck not only by how Iris taught me to look to the past but by how she insisted we look toward the future in our efforts to live and struggle and thrive in the present. This capacious vision has informed the tremendous scope of Iris's work as a community organizer, feminist activist, lawyer, filmmaker, and publisher. In all of these contexts, Iris creates space for the gathering together and amplification of Latina voices. This anthology is a testament to Iris's long-standing commitment to forward-facing community formation.

The Latinas whose voices resound in these pages speak out in a range of registers, accents, and genres. They break the strictures of form, they break the boundaries between languages, and they break the silence. In this way, they speak as Gloria Anzaldúa described, with forked tongues. For the Latinas whose words are captured here, the act of speaking is central to the articulation of selfhood and resistance, as Jennifer Maritza McCauley writes: "I am a rebel language."

Latina feminists along with other feminists of color have been instrumental in shaping our understanding of the body as a site of critical theory and liberationist thinking. From them we have come to name the weight we bear on this bridge called our backs or the refusals we make in our acts of *haciendo caras*. We have come to know how to live on this thin edge of barbed wire. Rosebud Ben-Oni asserts, "Brother, the blood / On my hands, Brother, / You are the home and I am the wilderness." The Latina writers and activists included here build upon the body of Latina feminist writings and construct new modes of embodiment as they struggle against the patriarchal constraints of the homes they leave behind or struggle to create.

The publication of this anthology is especially urgent in a moment marked by the "silence breakers" speaking out against sexual assault and the simultaneous silencing of women of color within these narratives. Latinas, in particular, have much to teach us as we face escalated attacks on Latinx immigrants, the U.S.-fueled crisis in Puerto Rico, and the misogyny that guides legislation against health care for women and children. The force of community forged here insists, as Emmy Pérez proclaims: "YES ALL WOMEN / on a crowded train and yes / all women and maybe / it was not okay."

Above all, the Latina voices that come together here, sing and shout and whisper and wail in lyrical conjurings. They beckon us toward a future where, as Aurora Levins Morales insists, we "must imagine an infinite river / of brown smiling children / who do not need documents / and a flag / of six billion stars." We follow the river, guided by the stars that are their words.

New York City
2017

Latina Activism

IRIS MORALES

Today Latina activists and artists are leading dynamic campaigns, projects, and grassroots movements to end systems of poverty and racism that are crushing the working poor, immigrants and families, LGBTQ and women of color. They are part of a growing political consciousness shaping a network of alliances among Latinxs, African Americans, Native Americans, Asians, Arab Americans, and progressive whites in the United States. Their demands challenge state and corporate power, broaden our vision of justice, and create possibilities for societal transformation. Yet struggles for economic and racial justice are largely invisible in the public discourse and generally ignored in the mainstream fight for women's rights.

Immediately after the results of 2016 U.S. presidential election were announced, women united to protest the anti-women politics promoted during the campaign. Latinas and other women of color assumed key leadership roles to organize a Women's March in Washington D.C. held on January 21, 2017. It was one of the largest political mobilizations in U.S. history galvanizing millions of women, men, and children of all ages to protest misogyny and the anti-immigrant, racist, and militarist direction of the new administration. At the massive gathering, prominent Latinas took center stage delivering fiery speeches and energizing cultural performances. Among them, actress America Ferrera set the tone in her opening remarks: "Our dignity, our character, our rights have all been under attack and the platform of hate and division assumed power yesterday . . . we march today for our moral core." Sister marches and rallies also mobilized in cities across the U.S. and around the world with crowds surpassing projected numbers. An estimated 2.6 million people participated in all 50 states and 32 countries,[1] displaying an exceptional outpouring of support for the rights of women, and for the rights of immigrants, African Americans, Muslims, LGBTQ persons and others targeted for hate by the administration.

Latinas turned out in big numbers. Not only to protest but also to articulate a vision of what we aspire to see in the world. This idea is at the heart of *Latinas: Struggles & Protests in 21ˢᵗ Century USA,* a collection of poetry and prose reflecting on women's lived experiences and the ways that Latinas address the relationship between gender and social change. The contributors are poets and activists, educators, artists, and journalists engaged in a variety of work from community organizing to university teaching. The selections illustrate how Latinas understand and resist the gendered conditions of their lives. They expose inequities that Latinas face as women but also by class; race, ethnicity, and national origin; immigration status; social location; and the legacy of history. The volume is most closely aligned with the view of feminism as "a movement to end sexist oppression, both its institutional and individual manifestations."[2]

Latinas: Struggles & Protests in 21ˢᵗ Century USA includes a mix of genres: poems, personal narratives, blog posts, letters, scholarly essays, artwork, mission statements, excerpts from plays, lyrics, and herstories looking across time, generational, and geographic boundaries. Each piece is unique. Together they open a window that reveals a range of Latina perspectives on important contemporary socio-economic-political and cultural issues, and imaginings for a more humane world.

WHO ARE LATINAS?

At the outset, it is important to emphasis that "Latina" is a "socially constructed" concept. In the 1960s, Chicana/Chicano and Puerto Rican activists in the U.S. used the terms "Latino/Latina" to signify similar histories and express solidarity with each other's social justice struggles. Later advocacy groups pressured to include a separate category in the U.S. Census to identify Latinos/Latinas, and the government settled on the term "Hispanic" in 1973 to recognize

---

1. Heidi M. Przybyla and Fredreka Schouten, "At 2.6 million strong, Women's Marches crush expectations." *USA Today,* January 22, 2017. https://www.usatoday.com/story/news/politics/2017/01/21/

2. "The Combahee River Collective Statement," http://circuitous.org/scraps/combahee.html

persons with origins in Latin America and the Spanish-speaking Caribbean.[3] (Until then, they had been assigned to the same category as "Whites.") The new classification—"Hispanic"—was, and continues to be, vigorously debated regarding the term itself as well as who is, or is not, included, and who decides. (The term Latino/a/x is used in this essay instead of Hispanic.) Nonetheless, the umbrella designation has served to recognize a national constituency that continues to evolve and represents a source, or a potential, for political power.

In 2015, more than 26 million Latinas lived in the United States.[4] This diverse population shares histories, cultural values, and languages but also has greatly different experiences based on social class, race, and immigration status. Several distinguishing characteristics are outlined here. For example, Latinas have lived in the U.S. for varying durations. They may be descended from immigrants who came to this country many generations ago, or they may be recent arrivals. Latinas are also descendants of the Native peoples who lived in the Americas before the European colonizers invaded—they are *not* immigrants. Puerto Ricans as U.S. citizens since 1917 also are *not* immigrants.

Generally, Latinas, documented or undocumented, migrate to the U.S. searching for economic opportunity or seeking refuge from political instability and violence in their home countries. In recent years, even thousands of unaccompanied children, including girls, have arrived at the U.S.-Mexico border. They make the journey alone fleeing horrific poverty, and political and drug-related violence.[5]

Latinas in the United States have roots in every Latin American country; the largest group is of Mexican descent followed by Puerto Ricans, Salvadorians, Cubans, Dominicans, Guatemalans, Colombians,

---

3. U.S. Census Bureau. Equal Employment Opportunity. https://www.census.gov/eeo/special_emphasis_programs/hispanic _heritage.html

4. Department of Education. *"Fulfilling America's Future: Latinas in the U.S., 2015"* https://sites.ed.gov/hispanic-initiative/files/2015/09/Fulfilling-Americas-Future -Latinas-in-the-U.S.-2015-Final-Report.pdf. 7.

5. Ian Gordon, *"70,000 Kids Will Show Up Alone At Our Border This Year. What Happens To Them?"* *Mother Jones,* July/August 2014. http://www.motherjones.com/politics/2014/06/child-migrants-surge-unaccompanied-central-america/

and others in lesser numbers.[6] Latinas may identify as natives of their home country or as Latina, or both. For example, the contributors to this book identify as Latina, but also as Chicana, Dominican, Mexican, Puerto Rican, San Salvadoran, Argentinian, Afro-Latinx, Afromexicana, and Boricua.

According to a 2014 study, the majority of Latinas in the United States were born in the U.S.,[7] spoke English and were fluent in Spanish.[8] Latinas may speak only English and Spanglish, a mix of English sprinkled with Spanish words. Latinas who speak only Spanish face steep language barriers and discrimination in getting jobs, education, housing, healthcare, and other vital needs.

While Latinas can be of all social classes, most are workingwomen. Disproportionately in the ranks of the poor and working class, they live within a complex set of pressures both as workers and as women. Of approximately 11.1 million Latinas in the labor force in 2015,[9] more than one-third worked low-paying jobs in the service sector in hotels, restaurants, casinos, household services, and childcare settings, and another third in sales and office occupations. About 25% held management, professional and related positions. Note that at every socioeconomic level, Latinas were paid substantially less than men.[10] Even Latinas with masters, professional, and doctoral degrees had the lowest median earnings of all racial and ethnic groups in the U.S.[11]

Racial differences and skin colors among Latinas span the human spectrum. The race dynamics in the Latinx community are multilayered and complex, and challenge the prevailing "white-black" racial binary of U.S. society. In general terms, Latinas confront

---

6. Antonio Flores, *"How the U.S. Hispanic Population is Changing."* September 18, 2017. www.pewresearch.org/fact-tank/2017/09/18/how-the-u-s-hispanic-population-is-changing/

7. Tanzina Vega, *"Most Latino Workers Born in U.S., Study Says."* *New York Times*, June 19, 2014. https://www.nytimes.com/2014/06/20/us/majority-of-latino-labor-force-now-born-in-us-study-finds.html?r=0

8. Flores, *"How the U.S. Hispanic Population is Changing."*

9. United States Department of Labor, Women's Bureau. *"Hispanic Women in the Labor Force."* https://www.dol.gov/wb/media/Hispanic_Women_Infographic_Final_508.pdfJ.

10. *"Fulfilling America's Future: Latinas in the U.S., 2015,"* 12.

11. Ibid.

systemic and individual racism and colorism (preference for lighter over darker skin color) as well as discrimination by ethnicity, class, and immigration status. Black Latinas are subjected to racism as Latinas, Afro-Latinas, and African Americans. Brown-skinned Latinas also confront racism based on skin color. Light-skinned Latinas face discrimination as an oppressed national, ethnic group. Because "whiteness" is promoted, both across Latin America and in the U.S., those who are seen as "white" have more advantages and benefit from "white skin" privilege. Latinas who can pass as "white" might choose to adopt whiteness and reject Latinidad altogether. The impact of racism, both in U.S. society as a whole and among Latinx people, is a central theme of the anthology.

COLONIZATION, SLAVERY, AND WOMEN'S RESISTANCE

Our shared histories as Latinas began the moment the Spanish conquistadores set foot on Caribbean beaches in 1492. There began the massacre of Native people that continued into South America. "The Indians of the Americas totaled no less than 70 million when the foreign conquerors appeared on the horizon; a century and a half later they had been reduced to 3.5 million."[12] The colonizers slaughtered an estimated 60 to 80 million Native people from the Indies to the Amazon,[13] and then they declared the Indigenous people *extinct*.

The European colonizers perpetuated another holocaust. They enslaved and exported Africans to every South American country from Brazil to Bolivia, from the Caribbean Islands to Honduras and North America. Though the precise number is unknown, scholars believe that the slave traders shipped 12.5 million Africans to North America, the Caribbean, and South America. 10.7 million men, women, and children survived the Atlanta Ocean crossing; but approximately 2 million did not.[14]

---

12. Eduardo Galeano, *Open Veins of Latin America, Five centuries of the Pillage of a Continent.* (New York: Monthly Review Press, 1973, 1997), 38.

13. David E. Stannard, Ph.D. "*Genocide in the Americas.*" *The Nation,* October 19, 1992, 430-434 http://www.skeptic.ca/Genocide_in_the_Ameri cas.htm

14. Henry Louis Gates Jr. "*How Many Slaves Landed in the US?*" *The Root.* January 6, 2014. http://www.theroot.com/how-many-slaves-landed-in-the-us-1790873989

The invaders committed mass murder and genocide. They seized the lands and looted its vast resources. They raped Indigenous and African women. Picture women running, screaming and crying in terror, trying to get away, fearing and pleading for their lives, fighting their attackers—millions of women over time. Desperation and despair drove some women to commit suicide and infanticide rather than suffer, or have their children suffer, the sadism and tortures of men.[15]

African and Native women were not passive victims. They fought back from carrying out acts of insubordination and destroying property, to poisoning the slaveholders and participating in uprisings and slave rebellions.[16] They also preserved and protected Indigenous and African cultures, passing on community values, traditions, and customs to their children.[17] Remembering and retelling stories from generation to generation was curative and healing, and is so to the present day. The horrors of colonization endure in our collective memory as the anthology's writers affirm.

By the 1800s, newly emerging nations in the Americas fought for independence from the Europeans. Women joined these struggles and expected that the triumphant leaders would grant basic rights to women; but they didn't. From then to the present, Latin American women have had to fight for access to education, labor laws, the right to vote,[18] and gender equality in all arenas. They have battled sexual violence and high rates of femicide.[19] Black, Native, and poor women relegated to the bottom of class and social hierarchies, suffered, and continue to suffer, most of all.

---

15. Karen Viera, *Powers, Women in the Crucible of Conquest, The Gendered Genesis of Spanish American Society, 1500-1600*, (New Mexico: University of New Mexico Press, 2005), 178.

16. *"Women In Resistance."* Slave Resistance A Caribbean Study. http://scholar.library.miami.edu/slaves/womens_resistance/womens.html

17. Melanie Byam, *"The Modernization of Resistance: Latin American Women since 1500."* *Undergraduate Review*, 4, 145-150. Available at: http://vc.bridgew.edu/undergrad_rev/vol4/iss1/26; p.1.

18. Julie Shayne. *"Feminist Activism in Latin America."* Encyclopedia of Sociology. Blackwell Publishing. Vol no. 4: 1685-1689. 2007. http://www.Julieshayne .net/Ency_FemActv.pdf 1685.

19. Virginia Sanchez Korrol. *"Women in Nineteenth and Twentieth Century Latin America and the Caribbean."* http://emsc32.nysed.gov/ciai/socst/ghgonline/ units/5/documents/Korrol.pdf

With the Monroe Doctrine of 1823, the U.S. government declared the Western Hemisphere closed to further European colonization, and the U.S. corporate elite took over. They exploited the laboring people, and financed dictators and regimes of savagery and torture to quash opposition. The resulting poverty and terror compelled Latinx people to seek escape and migrate from their home countries. In the case of Puerto Rico, U.S. colonial policies since 1898 have caused waves of mass migration so that today more Puerto Ricans live in the United States than in Puerto Rico.

Latinx arrivals find greater economic opportunities in the U.S. than back home, but they also suffer severe exploitation, language and racial barriers, and relentless police and state violence.

WOMEN OF COLOR FEMINISM

In the United States, the women's movement has its roots in the early resistance and rebellion of Native and African women. This long history is only briefly reviewed here.

By the 1800s, opponents of slavery were vigorously organizing for the immediate emancipation of slaves, and the end of racial discrimination and segregation. Out of this struggle also emerged a women's equal rights movement. Sojourner Truth, a former slave, an abolitionist, and a women's rights advocate, was a leading spokesperson addressing the inequalities facing both Blacks and women. In her famous "*Ain't I a Woman?*" speech delivered at the Ohio Women's Rights Convention in 1851,[20] Truth underscored the power of women: "If the first woman God ever made was strong enough to turn the world upside down all alone, these women together ought to be able to turn it back and get it right-side up again."[21] At the same time, she emphasized the racial divide and differences in the treatment of women, contrasting the chivalry afforded White women with the brutalization inflicted on Black women.

The 1960s opened a new chapter for women's rights in the U.S. African American feminists were again at the forefront fighting racism, sexism, and exploitation. Neither the Black Liberation struggle nor the women's movement responded to specific issues concerning Black

---

20. Sojourner Truth. *"Ain't I a Woman?"* December 1851. Modern History Sourcebook. https://sourcebooks.fordham.edu/mod/sojtruth-woman. asp

21. Ibid.

women's lives. Black male activists refused to recognize and address the "double jeopardy"[22] of racial and gender inequality, and the woman's movement focused primarily on the concerns of white middle-class women, failed to deal with both their class privilege and racism.

Like African American women, Latinas confronted similar experiences and barriers in the Latino and white women's movements. To fight for women's rights and social justice, Latinas mobilized in communities, workplaces, and schools, and led campaigns for economic and racial justice, affordable housing and healthcare, safe and legal abortions, and an end to experimentation with women's bodies. Puerto Rican feminists fought sterilization policies in Puerto Rico, which, by the mid-1960s, had resulted in more than 35% of women unable to bear children.[23] Across the United States, women of color joined in solidarity to stop sterilization of Native American, African American, Chicana, and Puerto Rican women.

Feminists of color also developed revolutionary ideas and frameworks that analyzed how systems of power operated. Identifying capitalism as the main oppressor, they described the multiple and intersecting dominations affecting women's lives by gender, class, race, and ethnicity—today known as intersectionality. Black feminists expanded on these ideas in the Combahee River Collective Statement written in 1977:

> "We believe that sexual politics under patriarchy is as pervasive in Black women's lives as are the politics of class and race. We also often find it difficult to separate race from class from sex oppression because in our lives they are most often experienced simultaneously. We know that there is such a thing as racial-sexual oppression which is neither solely racial nor solely sexual, e.g., the history of

---

22. Frances M. Beal, "Double Jeopardy: To Be Black and Female," in *Black Women's Manifesto* (New York: Third World Women's Alliance, 1969), 21-22.

23. Laura Briggs, *Reproducing Empire: Race, Sex, Science, and US Imperialism in Puerto Rico* (Berkeley: University of California Press, 2002), 83-87.

24. "The Combahee River Collective Statement," http://circuitous.org/scraps/combahee.html

rape of Black women by white men as a weapon of political repression."[24]

The women's movements of the 1960s and 1970s fought for the radical transformation of society and pinpointed the ways in which patriarchy and forms of male privilege were embedded in the practice of every political, economic, and cultural institution. These movements successfully challenged and transformed views about women, opened new opportunities, initiated groundbreaking laws, and introduced a broad range of social, cultural, and political rights enjoyed by women in the United States today.

LATINA ACTIVISM IN THE 21ST CENTURY

Despite the tremendous gains women have achieved, the struggle for gender and racial justice has not progressed far enough. Women still face violence, discrimination, and institutional barriers to equal participation in society. Zealous anti-women crusades have re-emerged that are eroding legal rights won in the courts, reducing workplace protections, decreasing women's health services, and minimizing claims of sexual violence. This well-financed backlash seeks to turn back the clock on women's rights.

Critically impacted by these politics, Latinas have mobilized and are organizing campaigns for economic and racial justice, affordable, quality education and health care, LGBTQ rights, an end to sexual violence, and other urgent social justice demands. With a clear stake in the outcome, they are striving to build organizations that include participation of women most affected by the issues—rather than the top down leadership structures of the status quo. Like prior generations, Latina activists are finding it essential to reclaim herstories for survival, develop collective strategies, and create coalitions to fight back. As the Combahee River Collective declared decades ago, "The most profound and potentially most radical politics come directly out of our own identity and oppression."

Latinas: Struggles & Protests in 21st Century USA reflects on themes emerging from women's lived experiences, and "on how gender has mattered and continues to matter—politically."[25] The

---

25. *Women Imagine Change*, eds. Eugenia C. DeLamotte, Natania Meeker, and Jean F. O' Barr (New York and London: Routledge, 1997), 3.

collection shows Latina activists expanding the feminist agenda, emphasizing the transnational nature of women's exploitation, and reaching out to women who have too often been ignored. Latinas are organizing women in low-paid, non-union jobs, linking women's and workers' rights, and recruiting new members into the labor movement. They are battling for improved workplace conditions and the end of the gender wage gap that pays Latinas an average of 54 cents to the dollar paid to white male workers.[26] Afro-Latinas are leading the fight against racism in Latinx communities in the U.S. and in Latin America. Inspired by, and in solidarity with, the Black Lives Matter movement, Latina activists are fighting police and other forms of racial violence. LGBTQ Latinas are at the frontlines responding to hate crimes and defending the rights of undocumented women and transgender immigrants. Latinas are exposing high incidences of sexual assault and violence in detention centers and prisons. They are also directing campaigns to safeguard reproductive health options for low-income women and families. Across the United States, Latinas are leading grassroots struggles for climate justice, immigrant rights, and decolonization.

Latinas: Struggles & Protests in 21st Century USA reaffirms the important role of Latina activism in the human rights struggle. The writings share dreams of a just world, the break down of hierarchies, and ideals of sisterhood. They imagine a different kind of future, of ways of living and relating to one another, and of organizing societies that are in harmony with the Earth and the needs of the people.

---

26. National Women's Law Center and Labor Council for Latin American Advancement (LCLAA). "Fact Sheet: Equal Pay for Latinas." http://lclaa.org /images/Trabajadoras_Campaign_2016/latinaequalpay_2016_english.pdf

PART 1.

WHO WE ARE

Raices/Roots

A Political Statement

KAREN JAIME

Someone once told me
that I was too political,
too radical,
that I needed to tone it down.
Why did I have to make
everything
into a political discussion?
Accept society's reality
as my own
and stop working to change it;
when my reality is what
I believe it to be,
not what you tell me it is.

I am a living,
breathing,
political statement
that refuses to fit into the box
you've devised for me
in your mental survey

I am not
denying who I am,
I'm just letting you know
that I don't fit
into your definition
of how I should be.

There isn't a word yet
that will encompass all of me
and provide you

with an accurate description of
what I am,
since you are basing it on stereotypes
brought to you by the media
and those that subscribe
to the "Latin Explosion Theory" of Latin@s.

Rest assured—
I don't have an ass like Jennifer,
hips like Ricky,
hair and eyes like Christina,
or a voice like Marc.
I am **not** that crossover poet
who will bring you knowledge
of foreign lands,
and make you feel
like you now know
what the Dominican Republic is like,
since *my* geographic marker
is on an Island
a train,
not a plane ride,
away.

I am **not** that person
that will sit here
and serve as your cultural translator
in order to further
your understanding
of the plight of urban youth,
when what you *really* mean is
ghetto rats
and how to get rid of them.

I am the undefinable,
the uncheckable,
the unmarkable,
that refuses to answer your question—

I am **that** Wild Womyn,
That see-line womyn,
That womyn
that doesn't sing the blues
and that leaves you wanting more.

I am your worst nightmare,
your biggest fear,
that which you did not think
was possible.
I am the impossible—
an endless possibility
because I refuse
to place myself into any of your categories...

I am like a blank page
waiting to be written on
by life's pen of experience.
My mere existence is political—
my loving womyn,
my speaking English,
my speaking Spanish,
my reading,
my performing,
my Dominicaness,
my Americaness,
my **everything** that is me
all wrapped up
in this brown skin
is political!

So don't ask me
to tone it down,
to not look at life
as what it is:
a long survey
with boxes to be filled in
when there aren't enough lines
next to it
to include all of the words necessary
to define me.

For to ask me to do so,
would be to ask me
to stop being me—

A living,

       breathing,

             political statement.

(First published in *Sinister Wisdom: A Multicultural Lesbian Literary and Art Journal*, "Out Latina Lesbians," Special Issue. Eds. Nivea Castro and Geny Cabral, 2015.)

Who Are We, Really?

GLORIA AMESCUA

We have so many names.
We are Mexican or Salvadoran or Guatemalan—
name any country south of the US border—
use it to name us who live here, born here or not.
Add American to it or don't.

We are the feared ones: scapegoats, illegals, burdens,
welfare cheaters, young women with a bunch of kids,
workers taking away jobs— in the shriveled hearts
of the scared and power hungry for so many decades
and still.

Over time and place, we have been called
Spics and Bean Eaters, Wet Backs and more.
Chicanos arose with the sixties and protests,
Hispanics with a government designation.
We are Latinos/as or Latin@ or Latinx,
trying to find a neutered name to encompass us all.

We are gardeners and teachers, lawbreakers and lawyers
We are housekeepers and judges, roofers and doctors.
We are dreamers dreaming and dreams fulfilled.

We have brown skin or black skin in variations
or we don't. We speak Spanish or English
or Spanglish or a native language or more than one.

What if we don't have memories of abuelas
passing on traditions or cuentos or dichos
or music or special foods or anything of a culture
left in the bones and ashes of older generations.

Who are we then?

We are who we say we are.

(2017)

Who Is Black?

Rosa Clemente

Yesterday, an interesting thing happened to me. I was told I am not Black.

The kicker for me was when my friend stated that the island of Puerto Rico was not a part of the African Diaspora. I wanted to go back to the old skool playground days and yell: "You said what about my momma?" But after speaking to several friends, I found out that many Black Americans and Latinos agree with him. The miseducation of the Negro is still in effect!

I am so tired of having to prove to others that I am Black, that my peoples are from the Motherland, that Puerto Rico, along with Cuba, Panama and the Dominican Republic, are part of the African Diaspora. Do we forget that the slave ships dropped off our people all over the world, hence the word Diaspora?

The Atlantic slave trade brought Africans to Puerto Rico in the early 1500s. Some of the first slave rebellions took place on the island of Puerto Rico. Until 1846, Africanos on the island had to carry a libreta to move around the island, like the passbook system in apartheid South Africa. In Puerto Rico, you will find large communities of descendants of the Yoruba, Bambara, Wolof, and Mandingo people. Puerto Rican culture is inherently African culture.

There are hundreds of books that will inform you, but I do not need to read book after book to legitimize this thesis. All I need to do is go to Puerto Rico and look all around me. Damn, all I really have to do is look in the mirror every day.

I am often asked what I am—usually by Blacks who are lighter than me and by Latinos/as who are darker than me. To answer the $64,000 question, I am a Black Boricua, Black Rican, Puertorique'a! Almost always I am questioned about why I choose to call myself Black over Latina, Spanish, Hispanic. Let me break it down.

I am not Spanish. Spanish is just another language I speak. I am not a Hispanic. My ancestors are not descendants of Spain, but descendants of Africa. I define my existence by race and land. (Borinken is the indigenous name of the island of Puerto Rico.)

Being Latino is not a cultural identity but rather a political one. Being Puerto Rican is not a racial identity, but rather a cultural and national one. Being Black is my racial identity. Why do I have to consistently explain this to those who are so-called conscious? Is it because they have a problem with their identity? Why is it so bad to assert who I am, for me to big up my Africanness?

My Blackness is one of the greatest powers I have. We live in a society that devalues Blackness all the time. I will not be devalued as a human being, as a child of the Supreme Creator.

Although many of us in activist circles are enlightened, many of us have baggage that we must deal with. So many times I am asked why many Boricuas refuse to affirm their Blackness. I attribute this denial to the ever-rampant anti-Black sentiment in America and throughout the world, but I will not use this as an excuse. Often Puerto Ricans who assert our Blackness are not only outcast by Latinos who identify more with their Spanish Conqueror than their African ancestors, but we are also shunned by Black Americans who do not see us as Black.

Nelly Fuller, a great Black sociologist, stated:

> "Until one understands the system of White supremacy, anything and everything else will confuse you."

Divide and conquer still applies.

Listen people: Being Black is not just skin color, nor is it synonymous with Black Americans. To assert who I am is the most liberating and revolutionary thing I can ever do. Being a Black Puerto Rican encompasses me racially, ethically, and most importantly, gives me a homeland to refer to.

So I have come to this conclusion: I am whatever I say I am! (Thank you, Rakim.)

(First published in the FinalCall.com, 2001.)

My Spanglish

PEGGY ROBLES-ALVARADO

The questionnaire asked me to indicate my primary language
I checked off other and in big, bold, blue bubble letters wrote in
SPANGLISH!

My Spanglish carries a Gillete under her tongue
ready to cut you if say she is the sister of ghetto Spanish
My Spanglish drops the -s and makes it ma' o meno'
switches the r with l pa no botal la suelte
trills her rrrrrrrs cuando tiene un pique rastrerrrrrro
and if you question the placement of her accent marks
she will replace them with side eye

My Spanglish gets in trouble for falling asleep in church
and winking at altar boys, climbs the fence at Highbridge
pool to swim after hours
My Spanglish burns her eyeliner with a lighter before applying it
My Spanglish can't stop sucking her teeth
My Spanglish knows the difference between
coquito and limber, pastelitos and empanadas, frío frío and piragua
Knows how to carry the weight on her thighs not her shoulders
My Spanglish cooks farina, tembleque, habichuela con dulce, arroz con
leche calls it comfort food

My Spanglish knows like lemonade-tamarindo was a popular drink and
it still is
Knows every Prince, Hector Lavoe and Fernandito Villalona song by
heart
My Spanglish wants to be called sexy, not cute
My Spanglish wants to be called smart before sexy, not cute
wants to be called beautiful like the blanquitas her ex parades
around the hood to show how he has moved up and on

My Spanglish mends her broken heart with bachata corta vena de
Frank Reyes
se emborracha con boleros del Buki
My Spanglish always claps when the plane lands safely
My Spanglish thinks freca, presentá y malcriá are all compliments
married her cousin to help him get his green card
doesn't let her kids sleep over anyone's house
My Spanglish has crooks and cops sitting at the same table
at her daughter's quinceañera
My Spanglish has a college degree and earned suma cum laude
in resting bitch face while riding the 2 train

My Spanglish is Washington Heights before the gourmet
fruit markets replaced C- town
before tomándose una fría in front of el building playing
dominó con los panas was loitering
before The New York Times and transplants from Minnesota
discovered pegaó on Buzzfeed and renamed it *"stuck pot rice"*

My Spanglish is Inwood before it became more affordable than
Williamsburg and was renamed Northern Manhattan
My Spanglish spray painted over billboards trying to rename
El condado de la salsa *"the piano district"*
wonders if it would have made more sense to name us
"The bomba y plena district", *"The home of hip hop district"*
or *"The boogie down district"* but my Spanglish is certain
The Bronx has always been and will forever be ART!

My Spanglish knows a fire escape is also a terrace
My Spanglish knows there is no way to heal without-
sana que sana culito de rana
can't tell stories about el campo in translation
can't flirt using proper grammar
My Spanglish knows there is no other way to say –
Cónchole papi, you look good!

My Spanglish has a tía sin papeles
My Spanglish has a tía that works in a factoría
My Spanglish has a tía that takes care of neighborhood carajitos
My Spanglish will never call herself broken

My Spanglish is an unwanted child who insisting on being born
She is huérfana crying an unpaid debt of commonwealth
to mainland lost in a promesa
Leche cortá of impoverished madre patria and starved island retreat
She is the unruly second generation daughter of un-American and un-standardized
She is the endangered tongue of a sanctioned homeland and un barrio cabrón
My Spanglish is always trying to create a bridge connecting
Quisqueya, Borinken and un verano en Nueva York

My Spanglish is a scared 7 year old in an English only class where
Ms. Marcy tells me to sit in a corner every time my tongue
resists pressing *ju* into you and *jes* into yes
insisting Mami's homemade lonches are better than cafeteria food
certain that standing on el rufo is the only place I have ever seen stars

My Spanglish has an Abuelito whose primary language is storytelling
but she doesn't have the time to sit and listen
My Spanglish can't understand all his consejos
but feels exactly what he means
when he says "Te amo, te amo all the way"

(2017)

When They Say Stop Speaking Ghetto

JENNIFER MARITZA MCCAULEY

I am a rebel language,

the wild bloodroot of
ancestral line.

I ain't gonna speak in
your cusses nor *cursivos*,
oye:

this talk
ain't school-taught,

it's ready for a gotdamn
brawl.

whatchu 'fraidofman
tienesmiedo,'mano?

what horrors could
possibly come
from these dumb,
dagger- words?

(First published in *Luna Luna*, 2016.)

I'm Your First World Problem

ROSEBUD BEN-ONI

I'm your benetton dream
    Gone rotten. Goodbye,

                    rhythm nation.
          I'm quite nasty on my own.
        I'm under bridges burning cash
    in aquanet bangs and riding pants.

        I owe the pleasure of this dream
        to your charitable vaccines
        to petting zoos that pop-up
        outside walmart
        where my yeshiva father sells guns,
        while my mexican mama
        spins your kids
        round-round
        in her 1099 part-time
        50 hours of grammar.

My anglo teachers still mark me
    absent on rosh hashannah.

                They slapped for spanish.

      I was paddled for every pro-drop
        and null-subject—

If only I'd gone pre-med or don the billboard
in toscani lens. Instead of greying mama's hair

at the ends and allan bloom
and harold too, great books, my friend,
where I hunt lawrence of mexico
under lowery's volcano.

For in the halls of great men I trespass
with elocution, with continental
accent. I snuck in
with nautical sweaters
and british spelling and bludgeoned
every headmaster.
I have taken the liberty
to open windows
of great halls, govern
every guvnor:
RELEASE THE HOUNDS
ON CORTÉS AND BURROUGHS.
Sometimes in tights from barney's warehouse
sale I aeroplane in sombre colours
across melville and hemmingway.
great anglos known to whale and sea
all to set sail
to a beautiful woman.
She is the one who will become the hall.
To her only I'll confess at twenty I had no money
and walked into saks in lifted joyce leslie
and I— was treated well.

I have the face of a young executioner.
I am the last temple,
the communal dressing room

where girls wear nothing underneath,
where you find yourself on your knees
offering up
both throat and key.

All the burdens in the world have just died,
and you're the last of your kind.
Turn around,
Bright
Eyes.

(First published in *Lana Turner Journal*, 2013)

[IM]Migration Journeys.
Crossing Borders.

A History of Walls

KARLA CORDERO

our home has a fence the color of dead blood. once my sister
launched her barbie into the neighbor's yard. while in flight the small
body stares back knowing it wouldn't return or at least not the same.
the next two days the sky poured out all its water. a plastic girl goes
missing & a wet tombstone is born.

my hometown rhymes with mexico & ends with a wall. a vertical
ladder built all wrong. & lays on its side like a sleeping mother
forgetting to feed her legacy. the children don't know how to wake her.
their bellies wail. mouths wide open. their tongues are a sea of small
pink hands reaching for the sky.

later i see on the tv screen an orange man to be president is now
president. when his mouth roars two rows of teeth become a violent
wall. a wrinkled forehead a mountain of walls. he thumbs up to an
audience. four fingers a caged fist. a prison. watch his thumb be
boastful border agent. counting the bodies he's collected.

(First published by *Tinderbox Poetry Journal,* 2017)

Border Hunting

NORMA LILIANA VALDEZ

Electronic sensors. Video monitors. Night vision scopes. Fiberoptic scopes. Horses. All-terrain motorcycles, bicycles, and sometimes snowmobiles. Over 109 vessels for marine patrol. Z Backscatter Vans. Digital fingerprinting. Optical/infrared cameras. Ground scanning radars mounted onto Ford 550 flatbeds. GPS coordinates. Tracking and sign-cutting. Re-con III thermal imaging binoculars. Webcams. Laser rangefinders. Towers with sensor packages. H&K P2000 pistols in .40 Smith & Wesson caliber. 12-gauge Remington Model 870 pump-action shotguns. .223 caliber Colt M4 Carbines. *Which one was used to kill Sergio Hernandez?* Helicopters. Drones. Airplanes. Mobile video surveillance systems. Underground sensors buried in the desert. Desert as weapon. Agents who chase and scatter migrants across hostile terrain. A vast graveyard of the missing.

(2017)

Grave Song for Immigrant Soldiers

AURORA LEVINS MORALES

José Gutierrez, José Garibay, Diego Rincón and Jesus Alberto Suarez were "green card soldiers" who died in Iraq and were given posthumous citizenship. Ezequiel Hernandez was shot in the back while herding his family's goats near his home in Texas by Marines taking part in border maneuvers.

Part I

I am sitting right here in California this
occupied land ripped with borders,
borders running like red scars
under the city limits and county lines
stitched into our hearts with crimson threads
a thick embroidery of grief
welts of damage criss-crossing
the everyday landscape of ignorance.

The wealth of the world may enter
but its people may not.
Industrial strength needles rise and fall
setting barbed wire stitches,
doing the meaty business of empire,
upon the hacked and reassembled body of the planet
drawing a bloody string through lives
that people living inside the gates
are instructed to forget

I am sitting here thinking Flor,
German, Lola, Manuel, Claudio,
Mercedita, Ricardo, Cristina, Ramon,
the stained gauze of foreignness
binding their fluid caribe tongues.

I think, how many Chinese women
were sent back yesterday morning
wrong papers start over
go back to sewing American flags
for six noodles a day
in mainland sweatshops
waiting for something new to happen.
I think Haitian bodies
dark driftwood on Florida beaches.
I think how many miles
from San Miguel to Tombstone
if you go on foot.

They are playing taps
for José, Diego, Jesus Alberto and José
worn in with their mouths taped shut,
obscenely wrapped in the prize
they could only win by
going in front, falling first, dying fast.
They have been given their citizenship
in the cemetery of the star spangled dead,
and their officers do not expect any trouble.
I tell them I cannot mourn you
in the small space they have set aside
in the margins of their blood road.
I must carry you with me.

I am thinking about Basra and the Alamo
about mayflowers and leaky boats capsizing
downstream from Port Au Prince, not pilgrims.
about Arizona vigilantes with assault rifles
patrolling an invisible line at the edge of their fear
that runs right through our living rooms,
terrified that Michoacan will conquer Colorado that bloodbath and
bankruptcy will come home to roost trying to hold their own history
at bay with equipment.

I am trying to see the faces of the
ten thousand unnamed bodies
fallen into the gullies and canyons
of the crossing, the ones that are never found and the two bodies a day
they do find strange fruit of the Mexican desert.

My great-grandmothers made lace,
twisting white cotton strands around pins
until the web could catch the sun, catch
a fall of jasmine down a wall,
delicate and tough, one thread bound into another,
spreading out across their beds and tables.
My great grandmothers wound pain
around pins and fingers.
They made lace out of suffering
and I am unraveling bandages,
pulling weft from the fabric of lies.
I am trying to twist this savage thread
around the pins of what I know,
fastening this to that,
fraying the edges of nations
to make a blanket.

I am making a shroud for immigrant soldiers,
knotting and tying a thousand
journeys to locked gates,
going under and around,
doubling back, knowing that someone
traveled by night,
wore a disguise,
carried false papers
swam the Ohio, the Mississippi, el Río Grande,
jumped a train,
crept through the sewers.
I am untwisting the sharp teeth of borders,
knitting rivers and veins in a fabric
as rough and fertile as earth,
the only cloth I can use
to bury you.

Part II

Someday the river
will be no more than a river
nothing but water
carving its way through earth.
Not a line drawn through our hearts,
not a place of execution, not
a floodground of smothered cries.
And those bones, those
ten thousand chunks of rough ivory tumbling restlessly along the
course of history,
will settle into the riverbed.

They will become the fossils
of an age that has ended. No one will remember
where the fences were
in what strange place the scorched
landing strips of an ancient ruthless war
were brought back
from the deserts of Kuwait
to make a deadly wall against which
people broke trying to reach bread.
School children will pause,
somber, trying to imagine what difference
there could ever have been
between one rough mountainside
full of snakes and coyotes,
and another, between your hunger and mine.

Listen José, someday jaguar will move like living flame
from Quetzaltenango to Yellowstone without hiding
in freight trains, without dodging guns, someday
America will stretch from Inuit dreams of
whales arched and gleaming under northern lights
and the crack of shifting ice, uninterrupted plains
where blue shadows chase each other across the wheat fields,

through red stone and grey-green brush smelling of sage
between volcanoes like a string of coral ember beads spanning the night
to where water spills down mountains, air thick and moist
with the smell of leaves opening, and the crimson slash of parrots'
wings copal rising, rain falling, river after river, grasslands again
to the last cracked rocks and icy seas of tierra del fuego
and there will not be one strand of wire, not one
hole filled with massacres, torn shirts bullets burned faces shoes
nowhere on the earth the boot marks of soldiers trained to make
orphans, no one alive who remembers what it was to eat garbage
in the streets of Guatemala City.

Listen, Ezequiel, herding
the ghosts of goats before the crossed hairs
of men devoured by their own weapons
until they see nothing but target,
bleeding slowly to death not
three hundred yards from your door, cooling
under the infrared eyes
of twenty-first century marksmanship;

Listen Diego, wrapped in an imperial advertising banner
halfway around the world from Colombia,
lying in your box between streets as shattered as
the world your family escaped,
where it is easier to buy bullets than beans,
and the most corrupt people in the world
the same ones setting up regimes
and toppling them with your broken youth
give lessons in assassination
and money laundering
to anyone who will deal in white powder,
for the wholesalers of desperation
pumping crack into the gaps
between be all you can be
and twenty years to life

making plastic chairs for twenty five
cents an hour in California prisons.
Liberation or a war on drugs,
its all the same, because
in your country, the dead
are the only ones who can object
without being gunned down.

listen citizens of the countries of breath
all of us illegal alien foreign uncivilized
savage beyond control
someday it will be enough to have been born.

But today,
while the world is still
a maze of borders and fences,
I will not mourn them with this blue
quarter acre of gated stars, this
harrowing of red and white
scratchmarks on the face of our continent. No,

in order to drape the graves
of four immigrant soldiers
shoveled in through the service door
while their starving relatives
stand outside the gates calling for food,

I must imagine an infinite river
of brown smiling children
who do not need documents
and a flag
of six billion stars.

(2003)

Refuge

FLORENCIA MILITO

after Orlando

Lands End. World-weary and diseased, we come fleeing the world's horrors. Our feeds bloated from the latest mass killing. A poet's tribute, the memory of boys dancing in her native Bahamas: swaying bodies, *purple shimmering wings.*

There's horror and there's our politicians' responses to horror, horror's horror: the crude, blundering xenophobia of the Bombastic Buffoon; the presidential calls for "ramping up" bombings and increased surveillance by Madame. On a runaway train we witness the twilight of Empire, its unraveling. But still there are bills to be paid, dirty clothes to be washed, toddlers with low-grade fevers demanding oatmeal with a small spoon, now.

Once the Yelamu Ohlone lived here. Here the edge where land meets water; jagged, monumental cliffs, a nagging feeling of vertigo. Here rolling sand dunes *deposited by wind and waves over thousands of years*, patches of wildflowers: mustard-yellow, purple, cherry-red. Here cypress groves and the blueness of the Pacific, ruins of old bathhouses. A line of birds. Beauty so disarming, so sweeping is difficult to apprehend; we are forced to parcel the landscape, or hide behind the camera lens.

Windswept, the cold jolts us out of our obsessions, cleanses the political toxins cursing our veins. Here looking down at the waves crashing against the rock, listening to foghorns in the distance, our minds wander to earthquakes, tsunamis. We become cognizant of endings, not in the mind, in the belly. There's duende here, a marriage of dark and light, a sense of our cosmos, of transience.

(First published by *92nd Street Y*, 2016.)

Los Boricuas

YSABEL Y. GONZALEZ

Flew over the States
saw how the roads below glistened,
I wonder if they listened to los santos'
whispering warnings:
your nose, too much like rising yeast
your hair, too much like black candied cotton
your skin, too much like flamboyán bark
would it have made a difference?

They walked streets that shined
from broken glass bottles,
laboring like ants
while grasshoppers played in blades of grass.
Worked factories, fireflies in the night
little lights shining through industrial windows.
Puerto Ricans really are amazing creatures
trading fantastic phosphorescent island bays
for diving in dumpsters.

Los Boricuas gave birth to our parents:
Young Lords and Aspirantes
who rushed boroughs to sweep streets,
birthed crayon flesh-colored boogie babies to fill cities—
never taught to use the machete buried in the basement.

And now, this generation invokes ancestry,
lights coal which glides over forged metal edges,
we gaze into the whitest part of Lady Liberty's eye
feel the pierce of her scepter,
wade in fire-worked implosions.

(First published in El Centro's online *Letras Latinas*, 2013.)

PART 2.

GENDER, CLASS & RACE

Intersectionality

"The concept of the simultaneity of oppression is still the crux of a Black feminist understanding of political reality and, I believe, one of the most significant ideological contributions of Black feminist thought."

Barbara Smith, Black feminist and scholar
Home Girls: A Black Feminist Anthology
(New Brunswick: Rutgers University Press, 2000)

The Poet's Response to #37 of John Baldessari's 109 Post-Studio Assignments

PEGGY ROBLES-ALVARADO

QUESTION: WHAT KIND OF ART CAN BE DONE WITH REAL ANIMALS?

When deciding what animal I wish I could
be my first thought was an elephant:
herding long distances with dust caking at
the tarsus, the largest matriarch leading
slow paced through the savanna, caring
for bulls that will one day leave me and call
it their nature to roam   My tusks yellowing
on an antique Steinway as scientists
rename my toothless kin adaptation

or maybe an impala: hunted for the
erotic measures of joy released in high
kicks, hind legs tempting rams even after
mating season   Trying to delay birth long
enough for my calf to hide in the herd as
lions call me prey, prop me between thirsty
canines for photographers who will
blame me for causing my own
graceful death

or maybe a viper with a sultry forked tongue
caressing hollow fangs hidden in the roof
of my mouth   A prism set behind each
slit- shaped pupil smelling the heat of
biologists setting traps, lurking until I
am tangled in fingers prying my jaw open

milking all my seductive with unwelcomed
persistent index and thumb   Leaving me to
soften and shed, birthing myself anew
or maybe I will wish myself woman
again   My erotic peddled into profane
My furies distilled, digestible
My evolution shrouded in myth like
Sirens, bleeding huts, Medusa, hysteria,
Sphinx   My waters: volatile and poisonous
My voice: tight fisted and
threatening like Mirabal Sisters,
Lorde, Assata, Anzaldúa, Lolita

and somehow I am told I must always
thank a man for a rib, a child, a proposal
a cat call   My anatomy pressing on
the opposing force that wants me to
quiet and bend   But as a beast of womb
and breast, as a creature of conjure
and contempt, I have learned women
are the art that can be made
of real animals

(2017)

Lines

Magdalena Gómez

in the cane fields you drove out serpents
with the flames of wild dancing;
in the mountains you outran incest
shred it with fingernails
gouged it with teeth.

eventually it caught you, Mami
and sold you at the market
next to onions and potatoes
where you pressed roses against your skin
alluring malaria to rescue you.

Mosquitoes ended their stinging
men did not;
they licked the fever
deeper into you
fever that pushed you
out of windows
into rivers
into walls;
fever that tempered
your soft spots into leather,
impenetrable skin that
repelled rain
and all thoughts of love.
fever in my blood
with every kiss
you pushed away,
offering instead
a little fist
of rice and beans.

you cleaned
all spills and broken things
into the shine of perfection
the mop, the broom
arrows against insults.

you learned to praise
other women's children:
the ones
with straight hair,
perfect teeth;
the ones
no darker than
an August peach.

you made your way
on trains
and always got two seats
one for your shopping bag;
de vez en cuando
you got lost
signs and maps
hurting your eyes.
you hated the smell of cats
and said so to anyone who listened.
you called all politicians liars
with wives who couldn't cook
assured yourself their children
surely must be drug addicts.
had your hair done on Saturdays,
made pin curls on Monday
to get through the week.
did laundry for the families
of the dead,
made *sopitas* for the sick,
made your own clothes
adding lace to church dresses

for the glory of God;
made Jesus out of dish towels
and rocked him to sleep.

Every night
you jumped off the edge of the world
in search of just one little dream
your mornings
full of nothing,
you slipped into your uniform
of faith,
sipping your coffee
like an heiress
knowing you once
drove serpents from the cane fields.

No man ever raped you deeper
than the English you didn't speak
your eyes collapsing
into dead birds
always in the presence of white folks.

if only we could go back
and I could
tell you the truth
about who they are
about who you are
and give you all the kisses
I saved
por si acaso.
if only we could rub ourselves in roses
simply because
they are beautiful.

(First published in Tea Party Magazine, 2005.)

Latina Workers and Allies Mobilized to Close the Gender Pay Gap and Promote Fair Work Conditions

Mónica Ramírez

Nearly one hundred organizations across the United States took action[1] on November 1, 2016, the national day of action for Latina Equal Pay, to raise awareness about the gender wage gap facing Latina workers. The most recent data reflects that Latina workers are being paid an average of 54 cents to the dollar paid to white male, non-Hispanic workers[2] This means that it takes Latinas 22 months to make the equivalent earnings that a white, non-Hispanic male worker is paid in just 12 months.

It is estimated that Latinas comprise nearly twice as many female workers than in 1994, increasing from 7.9% to 14.7%.[3] Despite the fact that Latinas represent a growing percentage of the labor force,[4] they are not necessarily more financially secure. In addition to equal pay violations, Latinas face wage theft, discriminatory job placement, failure to promote and train, job segregation and widespread sexual

---

1. Labor Council for Latin American Advancement "LCLAA Hosts National Event for Latina Equal Pay Day" http://lclaa.org/media/press-releases/press-releases-2016/889-november-1-2016-lclaa-hosts-national-event-for-latina-equal-pay-day

2. National Women's Law Center and Labor Council for Latin American Advancement (LCLAA). "Fact Sheet: Equal Pay for Latinas." http://lclaa.org /images/Trabajadoras_Campaign _2016/latinaequalpay_2016_english.pdf

3. US Department of Labor. "Hispanic Women in the Labor Force." (2015) https://www.dol.gov/wb/media/Hispanic_Women_infographic_Final_508.pdf.

4. US Department of Labor. "Labor force projections to 2024: the labor force is growing, but slowly." (December 2015). https://www.bls gov/opub/mlr/2015 /article/ labor-force-projections-to-2024 .htm

harassment. The situation is reported to be even more dismal for Latinas who are immigrants,[5] indigenous Latinas, and Afro-Latinas.

The Latina gender wage gap has a detrimental impact on the Latina worker and her family. Thus, equal pay for Latinas is not "just" a Latina worker issue. It is a family, children's, women's rights, labor and workers' rights issue that has consequences for our entire nation. When a Latina can not afford to put food on her table, a roof over head, save for her future or pay for her education or that of her children, this has a devastating impact for her, her loved ones, and our country.

We cannot view pay discrimination in isolation. This injustice is part of a larger picture of inequality, where the many facets of our lives –our sex, race, documentation status, level of education, and relationship status, among other factors, are used against us in an attempt to keep us from maximizing our potential.

Latina workers and advocates, like me, have been organizing for change for years. While it is true that Latinas are being undervalued, cheated and sometimes discriminated against in multiple ways at work, we are also powerful. We are taking measures to hold wrong doers accountable and determine our own future.

There are amazing trailblazers who many of us have grown up admiring and who have inspired our own activism, like Dolores Huerta.[6] She has dedicated her life's work to ensuring that Latina workers are not only counted as workers but also valued as human beings. In addition, other Latina labor leaders, like Aida Garcia, Dora Cervantes, Esther Lopez, Maricruz Manzanarez, Yanira Merino, Evelyn DeJesus, Maria Elena Durazo and many others, have been on the front lines organizing Latinas and other workers to stand up for fair wages and just conditions at work. There are workers[7] like an agricultural packing plant worker named Laura and Araclis, a shop steward at a hotel in New Jersey, who have bravely spoken out against gender discrimination and have stood up to assert their rights.

In addition, there are thousands of women who are leading campaigns, like our sisters at Restaurant Opportunity Coalition (ROC)

---

5. *See* Footnote 2.
6. See "About: Dolores Huerta." Available at http://doloreshuerta.org/.
7. *See* Footnote 2.

who are mobilized for "One Fair Wage"[8] and our hermanas at the National Domestic Workers Alliance[9] (NDWA) who have made significant advancements to increase protections for domestic workers at the state and federal levels.

Despite the odds, we are rising. We are rising up to speak out and stand up against unequal pay and all forms of oppression committed against our sisters, our brothers, and ourselves. We are grateful to the multitudes of organizations and individuals who stand with us today and every day. The future of our nation depends on the ability for all of us to be paid what we are worth so that we can succeed and thrive.

Find more information about ways that you can stand with Latina workers at www.latinaequalpay.org

(Originally published by *LATINA Style Magazine Online: LATINA Style Voices*[10] on November 1, 2016. Reprinted with permission.)

8. Restaurant Opportunities Centers United. "One Fair Wage Campaign: Kicks Off Women's History Month." Available at http://rocunited.org/2015/03/one-fair-wage-campaign-kicks-off-womens-history-month/

9. See National Domestic Workers Alliance. Available at https://www.domestic workers.org/

10. See *LATINA Style Magazine Online: LATINA Style Voices.* "Latina Workers and Allies Mobilized to Close the Gender Pay Gap and Promote Fair Work Conditions. (November 1, 2017) http://latinastyle.com/latina-workers-and-allies-mobilized-to-close-the-gender-pay-gap-and-promote-fair-work-conditions/

Infinite Grind

ANJELA VILLARREAL RATLIFF

(after *Tres Figuras,* a painting by María Luisa Pacheco)

Tres mujeres deep at work, arms broomed downward,
fists pounding masa on a long flat board. Braided
in their joint mission only the tops of their heads show,
black tresses pulled back, shoulders bulging from years
of labor. From the waist down, the diligent three fuse into
the cubist reds, blues, purples. Las tres become el trabajo!
Pacheco, the unseen fourth woman, poured herself into
this work . . . her modest moniker claims the canvas.

The bold strokes of La Paz's gifted daughter captured
Bolivia's indigenous pulse and the Andes' jagged polygons.

In *Untitled,* a brown and white abstract of earthen strata,
María Luisa nearly disappears into a left corner shadow
of *sin nombre.* Her visions prematurely halted
by a ravenous brain tumor. *I was not done with my
brushes, oils, my grand imaginings,* she may have
sighed. Her remains timelessly ambered for posterity.

(2016)

Defiant Chancleta:
The Power of Direct Action

IRIS MORALES

The men in my family had very strict views about gender roles. Men controlled the household and made all decisions even though their wives were strong and had jobs outside the home. Girls were at the bottom of the hierarchy and were referred to as *"chancletas"* or disposable slippers. Men like my father, who had only daughters and no sons, were ridiculed for being *"chancleteros"* or "slipper producers." Others would mock my father for having four daughters; he would squirm with shame and embarrassment. As I watched him, I felt demeaned and angry that he did not speak up for us "chancletas." I wanted to speak but did not yet know exactly why it bothered me so, and what I should say.

The men in my family would speak to their wives referring to me, "Her responsibility is to get married, to be a good wife and have children." I would get angry when I heard this; it was just assumed that I would comply. My mother, godmother, and aunts were the messengers. They worried about me. I came to hate any sentence that began, "To be a good wife, you must...learn to cook. To be a good wife, you must...fill the tub for your husband in the evening. To be a good wife, you must...fetch his slippers. I rebelled against the expectation that I would center my life on serving a husband and having children. I declared, "I will not do any of those things. Are men incapable of doing *anything* for themselves? Let him cook and fetch his own things," I insisted. For my opinions, I was branded, *"rebelde"* or rebel, and *"machua,"* which means like a man. My cousins were forbidden to hang out with me.

In school, I faced more barriers in the form of racism that questioned my intelligence and attempted to break my spirit. When I approached Miss B., the guidance counselor, about helping me apply to college, she informed me, in a serious and seemingly caring tone, "Unfortunately, my dear, you are not college material." I was shocked; I had worked hard since middle school when I had been truant and in trouble. I had turned around in high school, earned good grades, was elected student government vice president, and even had a role in the school play. But Miss B. insisted. "You'll *never* make it into a four-year college," she explained. At the time, the prestigious city university system of New York City offered free tuition, and each college required a high grade point average for admission. The mainly all white institution—students, faculty, and administration—enrolled only a few students of color, about 1.5 percent of the total according to pubic records. People of color at the college were the kitchen and janitorial employees. But, I had it in my head that I wanted to attend a four-year university. I was so angry with Miss B. for discouraging me that I cursed her over and over. I even wished her dead. Against her instructions, I went ahead and applied to the City College of New York as an evening, non-matriculated student.

A couple of weeks later, Miss B. died suddenly of a heart attack. As karma would have it, Susan, the student government president, called me and said that the school principal requested we speak at Miss B's memorial service to express our grief on behalf of the students. We went; we spoke, but I don't remember what we said. I know that we felt guilty. We had both cursed Miss B. and wished her dead on more than one occasion.

Immediately after high school graduation, I took a job at the West Side Block Association as a tenant organizer. Working out of a storefront office, I spent my days in the neighborhood knocking door-to-door, speaking with tenants about their housing conditions, organizing meetings, filling out legal forms, making court appearances and serving as a English/Spanish language translator. Several evenings a week, the tenant associations met to plan actions against greedy landlords and corrupt city building inspectors and to coordinate rent strikes. I loved organizing and became known around the neighborhood. Over and over, I witnessed injustices and racism, and how the legal system was stacked against the poor.

In one case, I went to court several times with Mrs. Perez trying to compel the landlord to deal with the rat infestation in the building where she lived. The first judge chastised us saying, "You can't just waltz willy nilly into this court claiming that there are rats in a building. The law requires proof; and, I don't know how it's done in *whatever* country you come from; but, here, in AMERICA, you have to bring evidence of your claim." So I asked, "How do we prove rat infestation? Kiddingly, I added, "Should we bring the rats to court?" "No, just the rat droppings," the judge responded seriously.

I couldn't believe it. I was outraged, but we went back to Mrs. Perez' apartment, collected rat droppings and took them to court. When we appeared before the judge, he asked, "Now how does the court know that the droppings are from the apartment that you claim? You could have collected the droppings from a construction site or any other place," he said. In my mind, I thought, "What a small man. Does he believe that we have nothing better to do with our lives than gather rat shit?" Out loud, I asked, "So how do we prove that the droppings are from Mrs. Perez' apartment?" "Bring in pictures," he instructed. "I'm sure you can find someone who has a camera and speaks English," he said condescendingly. The next time, the judge said that pictures were not good evidence because they could be doctored. We went back and forth with the housing court in this ridiculous and disdainful way; and, in the end, the legal system did nothing.

One morning, Mrs. Perez called me screaming hysterically that she woke up to find a huge rat crawling into her newborn baby's crib. Screeching at the top of her lungs, "I'm going to kill him! The landlord! *¡Lo voy a matar!* I'm going to kill him!" Believing her, I rushed to her apartment. When the landlord arrived a little later, I informed him that his life was in serious peril. "Mrs. Perez is going to kill you," I informed him. He immediately ordered the super to stuff poison and steel wool wire into the gaping rat holes and even replaced all of Mrs. Perez kitchen appliances with new ones. That day I wondered whether the legal system was pure evil or just impotent, but in any case, I learned the power of direct action.

Later that summer, I received a letter from City College of New York informing me that I was accepted as a student to start classes in the fall semester. Miss B must be turning in her grave, I thought.

(First published in *Bullying: Replies, Rebuttals, Confessions, and Catharsis,* Eds. Magdalena Gómez and María Luisa Arroyo, Skyhorse Publishing 2012.)

Where the 'Spicy Latina' Stereotype Came From–And Why It's Still Racist Today

Katherine Garcia

I am Latina. I am Latina. I am Latina. I feel as though I must reaffirm this to myself in order to truly believe it is my identity. Why? Because everything I see and have always seen about what it means to be Latina bears no resemblance to the way I look and the personality I present. Not only are my sexuality and the way I speak and dress not in alignment with the "Spicy Latina" stereotype, but my skin color and tight curls are also characteristics that tempt people to question my Latinidad.

I find myself fighting hard to validate my Latinidad to people who don't even know the difference between Mexican and Puerto Rican and really don't care to learn. Too recently I have been subjected to the following comments: "Wow, really? Are you 100% Puerto Rican or just half?" "You don't really look Puerto Rican." "But, you don't even have an accent." And my favorite, "Say something in Spanish!" Or even worse, "Say something in Puerto Rican!" Often times I find myself saying, "My mom is Puerto Rican, that's why I'm so lively and colorful," with the same enthusiasm as April Ludgate from *Parks and Rec*.

Seriously though, this stereotype and the clumping of all Latinas into one massive bowl of sameness doused with way too much extra spicy hot sauce is a real problem. It objectifies us and makes our multidimensional awesomeness invisible to society and to ourselves, especially when we attempt to drown out our individuality to fit neatly into the "Spicy Latina" box. This stereotype is so pervasive and ingrained into our perception of Latina identity that we have all been exposed to it. To better understand it, we must first unpack its history and the ways it has manifested itself in our everyday lives.

HISTORY OF LATINX MARGINALIZATION

So how exactly did the Spicy Latina stereotype form? To answer this question, we have to go back to 1846 during the Mexican-American War. I know it seems far-fetched to go this far back but hear me out because there is a connection. The Mexican-American War was a struggle to stop further United States expansion into Mexican territory; and, although political divisions within Mexico led to a U.S. victory, the consequences of this war extend beyond the loss of land.

The most powerful weapons utilized in war are manipulation and racist ideology, and this war was no different. The idea of "Manifest Destiny" in particular helped justify invasion and violence. Although to the U.S.-American people, invasion seemed best for all; it was really only best for them. As the dominant group, they had the power and resources to influence public perceptions of the Mexican people. Journalists and content creators painted Mexicans as a lazy, corrupt, and disappearing people. So what did this perception lead to? What it always does, erasure and major oppression. The blurring of Mexican identity and experiences allowed for the formation of stereotypes like the Spicy Latina.

CREATING THE IMAGE OF CHIQUITA BANANA AND OTHER FUCKED UP MEDIA REPRESENTATIONS

The media portrayal of Latinx people has been offensive at best. This is something Latin American countries are not oblivious to. In fact, Mexico called for an embargo of U.S. films in 1922 because of the messed up image they painted of Mexican culture. In 1933, this portrayal changed slightly. To be honest, the new image still had major issues; it was just serving a different agenda.

In 1933 President Franklin Roosevelt announced his "Good Neighbor Policy" that did succeed in making Latin America and the United States friendlier neighbors. The temporary peace was beneficial for Latin America because it ensured that the United States stayed out of Latin America's business, helped economically through filmmaking that promoted tourism, and created more opportunities for work in Hollywood. Sounds like a sweet deal, right? Sure, except, not really. See, the United States needed Latin America on their side during WWII. Talk about ulterior motives. So, yes the United States did help with filmmaking and promoted tourism. The problem was that this new image replaced negative stereotypes with more (friendlier) stereotypes. The new image was still not true to the diversity and unique cultures of Latin American countries.

One of the most popular icons that emerged from this policy was the Brazilian dancer, Carmen Miranda. This Brazilian Bombshell was the Spicy Latina stereotype personified with her exotic Latin accent and emblematic fruit hat. She lives on to this day as the perfect example of "Tropicalism" or the portrayal of Latin Americans as exotic, fun, and friendly foreigners. She was so much the symbol of Latin culture that the United Fruit Company created Chiquita Banana, a cartoon character whose resemblance to Carmen Miranda was no coincidence, to represent their company.

So what exactly does the Spicy Latina look like? Let's start with the physical aspects. When I do a simple Google search, it conjures up images of olive skinned, raven haired, red lipped, curvaceous women. It's no surprise that the first is Carmen Miranda, the epitome of the Spicy Latina herself. My eyes quickly shift to a colorful image of a pulp fiction novel titled *Spicy Adventures: She Devil* featuring a scantily clad, olive skinned, raven haired, red lipped, curvaceous woman. Then there is a picture of the actress Michelle Rodriguez seductively holding a gun, then one of the actress Sofia Vergara on the cover of *Esquire* magazine with the word "sex" emblazoned over her lower half, and a picture of a spicy chicken sandwich next to another of a *Saturday Night Live* character portraying a Latina. Most other images are of women with skin-tight clothes, light skin, and straight or wavy hair.

ACCORDING TO THIS SEARCH, LATINAS ARE SYNONYMOUS WITH SEX AND SPICY FOOD.

What about personality, you might ask? A Spicy Latina must be loud, bombastic, and seductive (insert sexy Latin accent here). She must also be hot-blooded, quick-tempered, and passionate. Think Gloria from *Modern Family*, or Gabrielle from *Desperate Housewives*, or Eva Mendes in…well, everything. In fact, think of any Latina character in the media and chances are if she is not portraying a feisty maid, she is portraying a Spicy Latina.

Although the Spicy Latina is an object of desire, she may have too much personality to handle. So much so that she is viewed as domineering or emasculating. This positions the man as a bullfighter who is applauded if he succeeds in taming and conquering the bull.

Of course, the main appeal of the Spicy Latina is her sexuality. She is extremely sexy. She is lustful, promiscuous, and tempting. She is also very clearly heterosexual. These dangerous and irresistible vixens use their physical assets to lure and catch their mates. If they can't bait you with their bodies, then they will tempt you with their food. Spicy

Latinas know the way to a man's heart is through his stomach. They don't just love sex and want to have it all the time; Spicy Latinas are sex. Once they have trapped you, they will fulfill all your sexual desires because they are willing to do anything to make you happy. After all, Spicy Latinas exist only for your pleasure and entertainment.

Why is this image so fucked up? I mean, there are worse things to be associated with than sexy, beautiful, and passionate—right? Let me explain. Being called a Spicy Latina is like being called a delicious spicy chicken burger. I have certain expectations when it comes to my burgers, and I will be highly disappointed if they are not met. The problem, if it's not obvious yet, is that Latinas are not food! I am not juicy; I am not a hot tamale, and I am definitely not spicy. Without going around and asking permission to taste the Latinas I know, I think it's safe to say that none of them are spicy either.

IT'S WONDERFUL TO BE THOUGHT OF AS SEXY, BEAUTIFUL, AND PASSIONATE, EXCEPT FOR WHEN YOU DON'T HAVE A CHOICE.

The problem with the Spicy Latina stereotype is that it generalizes Latina identity and doesn't allow room to form an individual and authentic self. This overgeneralization of Latinidad makes it hard for Latinas to see themselves as anything but what others expect. It is a form of oppression that aims to limit potential through the internalization of an image. This exoticism and fetishizing of women's bodies transforms Latinas into mere objects. They become less human and more like prizes to be won and showcased.

Although there has been some improvement (*Ugly Betty* and *Jane the Virgin*), there is still a huge issue with typecasting in Hollywood. When the only roles Latina actresses have available to them are the Spicy Latina or sassy maid, then that is all the public sees; and, all the public expects. These are also the role models available to Latina girls. If their role models are never the doctors, never the teachers, then young Latinas do not see these as attainable goals.

Other reasons why the Spicy Latina stereotype is so fucked up have to do with race and sexuality. Latinas don't all look the same as represented in the media. There are different races within Latin America (shocking, I know). Yet, because I don't look stereotypically Latina, I find myself having to explain that even if my skin is darker than my sister's, I am not any less Latina. Just because my hair is big and curly, and not at all like Jennifer Lopez's, doesn't make me any less than 100% Puerto Rican. The exclusion of Afro-Latinas in our society is painfully obvious. Rarely do I see Latinas, "spicy" or otherwise, who look like me in the media.

Moving on to sexuality. What if you are a Latina who does not identify as heterosexual? What if you identify as lesbian, or bisexual, or asexual? Sorry, you do not fit into the Spicy Latina box. As mentioned earlier, one prominent characteristic of the Spicy Latina stereotype is her sexuality, or more specifically, her heterosexuality. This is coupled with the societal and family pressure to reproduce, and the belief that all Latinas are or will someday be mothers because they are too sexually promiscuous not to be.

As a bisexual identifying Latina, I resent this. It took me so long to accept my sexuality because everything I saw and was told about being Latina was that I should be attracted to men only, that I should dress for men only, and that my ambitions in life should ultimately lead to motherhood. I'm not saying there is anything wrong with these things, as long as you are happy and don't feel you are betraying your identity. But, unfortunately, it's not like that for too many of us.

The Spicy Latina stereotype is fucked up for so many reasons, but the saddest part is that others think they have the authority to question if you are Latina enough.

Truth is, I am Latina enough for me, and I don't need anyone's permission to be.

(First published at http://everydayfeminism.com, 2015.)

Reclaiming Indigenous & Afro-Latina Identities. Fighting Racism.

Volver, Volver

ARIANA BROWN

y volver, volver
to the mouth of the Yucatán
where we first glistened
with a stranger's tongue,
Spanish,
our old muscles bullied into
lovely wrecks &
our mothers wept
at the loss, for
they knew language
is the last sound
of war; & then
came the trumpets

volver
a tus brazos otra vez
my grandmother's
elementary, her inherited
Spanish trickling through
closed lips, as the teacher
instructs, 'English only';
& my grandmother
is an essay
on shame, a grito
trembling the walls
the color of sorrow

llegaré hasta donde estés
four years of Spanish classes
to remember the name
of grandmother's tears;
learning first

to pronounce each
syllable with the intent
of a conquistador - if
I am to grieve properly,
give me my language with
which to do it

yo se perder, yo se perder
black as a young moon, I
am spoken to in English,
the third tongue, final
conquest, never mistaken
for indigenous, never pain,
never daughter of woman
who hums mariachi songs
in crowded restaurants,
skimming lyrics in favor
of memory; & all I want
is permission to love
the gaps in my lineage
as one would the breaths
in a favorite song

quiero volver, volver
volver
& when our tongues spin
in ways we don't understand,
I open the ancient faucet, let
memory guide this
new music until it is
the shape of something
I can hold,
close, like a prayer,

& I forgive the chaos
violence has left me
& I worship my
flexible sound
& I kiss my lover
with the mouth
I own.

(First published in *Kweli Journal,* 2016)

"Volver, Volver" is a famous mariachi song popularized by Vicente Fernández.
The chorus appears sequentially in the poem
as the first italicized line of each stanza.

La Gruta

Liliana Valenzuela

Para Sandra

Chorro de agua
on my baby soft spot
en la mollera
volcanic water
hot womb
surrounds my dried body
chorro
purifícame
chorro
despiértame
chorro
bendíceme
eighty tons of water
pounding my crown
tired back
achy hips
opening   opening   opening

Back to El Bajío
the Mother Land
donde mi mamá nació y creció
the earth still heats up
this magma water

II
We sing in caves
echo one another
La Bella Durmiente
an aria in your soft tremolo
O sole mío
Farolito
In this primordial space
Waters Heal
muscles let go

somos amibas
aguamalas
nenúfares
esta bóveda de piedra
    encircles us
we line up
among the old and the newly young
waiting our turn

chorro on heart chakra
these changed breasts
water massages my rump
hips, thighs, neck,
I let go
breath finds me
    washed ashore

III
I float back
on this birth canal
light filters through
palm fronds
pirul
I come out onto a larger pool
float adrift   lighter than sound
the body remembers

(San Miguel de Allende, México,
Feb. 2, 2016, Día de la Candelaria.)

Diosa

MAGDALENA GÓMEZ

Luisa caught the fiebre
passed down from her
tatara tatara tatara güela
brain fever
that kills all the *pobrecito*
excuses for liars
zánganos y *comemierdas*
she will not do *limpiezas*
on sunny days
or cook for *exigentes*
or wear *fajas*
or *brasieles con alambres*
so she is mistaken
by some
as a privileged gringa
by others
as an *engreída*
by some
as an *hija de su madre*
(which she is)
and still by others
as the reincarnation
of Atabex

In bars
at board meetings
in church
in school
at the market
in bed
at the park
in restaurants
she writes on napkins:
"Know me or p'al carajo"
and leaves the imprint
of her mouth.
She is a coconut
making work
of being tasted.

(2011)

Because Brown Women's Bodies are Told We Take Up Too Much Space and When I Inhale I Make Sure It's Breath I Need

YSEBEL Y. GONZALEZ

*

My chest expands shallowly to keep my heart pumping
and when I exhale I consider my breath's direction
and the path it takes to reach everyone within five miles.

*

Yes, it's a lot of work, sparing the world. We impose
when we appear (at your grocery store, salon, laundromat, crosswalk)
when we shouldn't.

*

And I'm like every brown woman you've ever met,
difficult to make space for us even when we accommodate,
even when we peek our heads into ugly little rooms double-checking

that we'll fit.

*

Conserving breath is a brown art, which we've mastered—
my perfect English won't save me now.

(2016)

What to do when your renowned Mexican poetry teacher points out exactly where in your poems you sound like a tourist in Mexico

NORMA LILIANA VALDEZ

Go to the nearest taqueria and order tres de costilla and a Victoria.
Buy a Tehuana huipil in cobalt and black.
Make plans with your friend Tonatiuh to eat mole at a stranger's house on Friday night. Trek the side of a mountain and visit an Aztec pyramid.

Remember you speak Chicana fluently. Remember you've shaken Dolores Huerta's hand and drunk mezcal with Sandra Cisneros.
Read Gloria Anzaldúa, again.

Remember your grandfather was a bracero, which means there was not enough food. Remember your pregnant mother rode a bus for two days to get to the Tijuana border. Remember your father was deported at least once.

You did not speak English when you started kindergarten.

Remember you know how to clean the spines from nopales, how to palm corn into tortillas and tamales.
Remember your unborn brother buried under the milpa. Remember your great-grandfather,
your grandmother.

Say their names. Nieves Ornelas Romanita Ornelas
Say your name. Norma Liliana Valdez
Who you come from,
Maria de los Angeles Ramirez y Juvenal Valdez and where.

(2017)

If Cain the Younger Sister

Rosebud Ben-Oni

My brother is a whitewashed synagogue.
His words are mud-bricked and windowless.
From desert frond and dust he builds a home.
A man of principle, my brother
Remembers the Alamo.
He tried to guide me
Training-wheel free
So I wouldn't fall
For men like Crockett or Koresh.
He promised I was a complete
Mensch and mother's family too,
Ofrenda of flower, skull and bread.
At ten he solved a dispute
By reciting Kaddish
On the Day of the Dead.
My brother would bury me if he had to.
My brother would build me a coffin
And nail it shut. To this day
He turns down the radio
Passing burial ground.
I never showed that kind of respect.
At sixteen I totaled his car
Outside Seguin
Looking for another city.
In the ER, mother screamed
And the nurse had no
Sympathy. I nearly
Killed a man.
I never confessed
I saw him coming
And careened
At full speed.

Never again
Will my brother sleep.
He locks the doors
And waits for me.
Every night tympanis
Buried in the vistas
Awaken me. I emerge from
An ark covered in marigolds,
A feather child leaving her ossuary.
I died in the Indian laurels of San Agustín.
Brother I'd like to have said brother
You are the fort and I am the death wish,
Sacrificing all
At last stand.
Brother, the blood
On my hands. Brother,
You are the home and I am the wilderness.

(First published in *So to Speak*, 2013.)

When Trying to Return Home

JENNIFER MARITZA MCCAULEY

In the morning, I leave a panaderia on SW 137th
and a Miami browngirl sees my face
and says de dónde eres Miami or Not?
And I say Not, because I live in this blue city now
but she means where are your parents from
and I tell her I have a Daddy who is Lou-born
and coal-dark and looks like me and I have a Mami
who is from Puerto Rico and looks like the trigena
in front of us who is buying piraquas for her yellow children.

The browngirl says eres Latina at least, and I say at least
in English. I look down at my skin, which is black, but
smells blue by the shores of Biscayne. She thinks my skin could
speak Spanish, a los menos. I want to tell the browngirl I was not born
by ocean rims or white-scuffed waves. I was not born
beside browngirls who speak Miami's itchy Spanish. I was born
where my culture rarely bloomed—amongst Northern steel-dust and
dead skies, where my two-colored parents stuck out at any
Pittsburgh party. I want to tell her, I would love to be the type of girl
that says soy de Somewhere and everyone says, "Girl, I see"
or "you're una de las nuestras"
or "you belong."

I want to tell her, you are right, in this blue city, I look like everybody
and everybody looks like me, and this is the thing I've always wanted:
to be in a crowd where nobody remembers my skin. I've wanted
this when I was a child, amongst grey buildings and steel-dust
where they called me unloved and weird-colored but here, mija,
I smell like blue and people who look like Mami can say funny
things like at least, at least.

Instead, I smile at the browngirl and she does not smile back.
Instead she says, in Spanish: If you are Latina, you should be so,
speak Spanish to me. And I say, in English: Yes, I could
but I am afraid, and she laughs in no language and judges me.

I want to tell her the history of my family-gods. They are rainforest-hot,
cropland-warm, dark with every-colored skin. They have mouths
that sound like all kinds of countries. I want to tell her these gods
live wild and holy in me, in white and blue cities where my skin
is remembered or forgotten, in cities where I am always one thing, or
from anywhere.

I want to tell the browngirl this while she turns and walks off.
I want to tell her that when she came to me, thinking I was hers
in that moment we were together,

at least.

(First published in *Aspasiology,* 2016.)

Afro-Latinidad and Redefining Resilience in the Latinx Community

AMANDA ALCANTARA

When I think of resilience one of the first things that comes to mind is the burden that so many of us carry as people of color that forces us to be resilient, otherwise we will remain under the concrete.

When I think of resiliency, I think of the fact that Afrolatinx are alive in Latin America. That my curly hair and olive skin survived the transatlantic slave trade and colonization, and constant messages from white supremacy that I have to straighten, whiten, *thinnen*, hide myself, and so many parts of who I am, and who we are as the descendants of one of the worst crimes in humanity.

But before I got to this understanding, a lot had to happen within my consciousness. When I was a little girl growing up in the Dominican Republic, I remember someone called me "*morenita*." My response was, "*Yo no soy morenita; yo soy india*," which translates as "I'm not Black; I'm Indian." The myth of *mestizaje* and reclaiming of indigeneity to serve nationalist and *independentista* purposes from previous centuries somehow managed to survive to the late 1990s and early 2000s when I had already learned that to be Black was a bad thing. So I lived almost disconnected in this body, internalizing self-hatred, and learning that the best things about me were those closest to "whiteness."

The Afrodescendents of the Dominican Republic and many other Latin American countries have this experience. It's Blackness denied by the state because Blackness cannot exist without being in direct resistance to what the state unfortunately continues to uphold: capitalism and white supremacy. And while denial of Blackness is one of the things that many AfroLatinxs speak of, the truth is, there is a denial of humanity and dignity tied to this as well. This is what I mean by Blackness being in direct resistance to the state.

Black people in Latin America are among the poorest across the continent. There is displacement happening in Afro-Colombian communities; chemical studies against people still taking place in Puerto Rico; anti-Haitianism across the continent and an

73

unwillingness to say that racism is the cause—because of, again, the myth of mestizaje—that is, that we are all somehow a joyous amalgamation of different races living together in harmony.

We're not.

Although there is a harmonious way in how sticks caress drums to the sound of the Spanish guitar to create salsa, and in the way in which rice and beans are so perfectly complimented by sweet plantains, the African-influence in these dishes and our music are practically invisible in the larger narrative of Latinidad. We don't celebrate Afro-Latinidad.

In one of many conversations at a Rutgers University dorm during my undergraduate career, my friend explained why I wasn't included in the Latina label, and why this dislike of Dominicanness existed in Latinx culture. She told me, "They don't like us because Dominicans are Black." Immediately it all clicked; it made sense. I could see that things disliked about Dominicans that I thought were tied to a culture of joy, a culture of resistance, a culture that embraces music and speaks loudly with mouth wide open as if every word is the beginning of a song, were seen by others as synonymous with a warped, negative view of blackness. Recently, I've taken to call myself Black or afrodescendiente instead of Afro-Latinx because "Latinx" doesn't even represent me.

And this doesn't only happen to Black Latinxs; the truth is Black and brown struggles are deeply tied.

Within Latinidad, it is common to celebrate European descendancy to separate from other people of color. Sometimes indigenous heritage is celebrated, but only as hyper-nationalism, and as a gimmick—like during el Día de la Raza known in the United States as Columbus Day.

The issue is that when we speak of or attempt to celebrate the resilience of the Latinx community, Black and brown folks are often excluded. When we speak of resiliency, we must recognize this disparity. I say, let's include the elderly man who is working selling *paletas* way past what is deemed a retirement age; the Black Latina teacher making a difference in students' lives by encouraging them to be their best; the little girl who is told she is Latina but doesn't see her afro or dark skin represented in the media or in the farm workers and laborers across the continent.

You see, people who are born with privilege, those not living in poverty, don't need to be resilient—they have connections, and if they're white, they don't have negative stereotypes attached to them. From a young age, they go to schools with resources dedicated to putting them on a path to success. They are financially in a better place. Their contributions to society are recognized, whereas the contributions of Black and brown folks aren't.

When I came back to the United States, and I say "back" because I was born here but left at the age of three, I wanted to believe that working hard was enough, that fighting was enough. I wanted to believe that just being positive was enough. Believing that is often easier than accepting that our community is under assault. But my dreams were naïve, and they shattered when I found myself sleeping on my sister's couch after college, even though I thought I had done everything right. I had a good GPA; I graduated from a good school, did two internships, spoke three languages fluently, and worked in the school newspaper, and TV and radio stations. I thought I could earn my humanity by sticking to the books, but I was wrong.

Pain is often romanticized and resiliency with it. Some say you must hit rock bottom to go up or that suffering and hardship make one stronger. For people of color, there is no choice. If you want to get ahead, you have to be resilient. If your family is already in a good place, it's because someone in the past was resilient. You have to work twice as hard; you have to get through hoops; sometimes you have to assimilate—and if you spend enough time in spaces away from home, you do change and have to fight to stay true to your roots.

So I invite us to redefine resiliency.

I have been thinking about my grandmother a lot. She passed away in 2012, the night after I graduated from Rutgers and received my undergraduate degree.

There's this saying that everyone knows in Latin America, particularly everyone from Caribbean countries. You may not be Black pero "¿ y tu abuela?" But is your grandmother Black?

When I think of my grandmother, I can't come up with a better example of someone who was Black and resilient. Usually examples of the rose that grows from concrete are college graduates like myself and first generation doctors and lawyers or persons who own property. Regrettably, we only think of those who "get out of the hood."

But others like my grandmother are roses too. She fed everyone every night in her home and caressed me softly while singing as she put me to sleep. I direct my attention to those people, Black and brown folks who have been excluded from the construction of Latinidad, the ones in struggle, the ones who are undeniably Black and know it, the ones who might have been taught to deny their Blackness, and yet are unapologetically Black in their actions and words and culture and music and dance and sometimes even their politics. I direct my attention to people of color from Latin America; the *señora* selling mango with chili by my job in Union Square; the single mother collecting food stamps whose image is used by conservatives to perpetuate negatives stereotypes against us; yet she is in many ways the backbone of our communities.

Resilience is in us because it must be.

I want to celebrate the resilience that exists simply because it can, even in moments when we are okay, even when a payment was made on time, and we get into the school of our choice, and dad gets out of work early. I want to celebrate the resilience that comes from within and the fire that exists in us because we are a people who celebrate life so powerfully and majestically, not only who excel in difficulties.

As we continue pushing for our community to be free of the shackles of colonization, let these moments be the main course—let this loving resilience be what helps us heal; let this resilience lead us in the path towards a better future and liberation.

(This is an excerpt from a speech written in 2016.)

Statement in Support of Black Lives

MUJERES UNIDAS Y ACTIVAS

Mujeres Unidas is a group of Latina immigrant women with the dual mission of personal transformation and building community power. Among our core values are compassion, learning, and solidarity. . . . We call upon those core values to guide us in our work and to drive how we want to be in relationship to other communities seeking justice. We recognize the importance of standing with our Black brothers and sisters in this crucial moment as well as long term in our shared fight for liberation.

As immigrants to this country we understand that our acts of solidarity must go beyond simply proclaiming Black Lives Matter. We must take a hard look at ourselves and motivate ourselves to learn about the history of the place we have come to live. We must study and deeply understand not only the history and legacy of racism but also specifically anti-Black racism and the ways in which we as immigrants both benefit from and are harmed by it. We must recognize the ways in which we are impacted by systematic racism as immigrants, but also the ways it uniquely attacks Black people and communities.

Our understanding must also extend back to our home countries —to the history and legacy of slavery and racism there and the ways in which we deny, erase and disparage blackness and our own Black heritage in our families, communities and societies. We must understand how anti-blackness is embedded into our language and our social structures and how detrimental that is to all of us.

It is our responsibility to share what we have learned with our friends and our families, with our children and our neighbors, to have conversations that may be difficult but are necessary if we are truly committed to creating a just world.

With humility and love we recognize that we have a big learning curve as we lift up Black struggle. We understand that our silence is complicit and that complicity is deadly. There is an urgent need for us to join our voice to the millions of other voices screaming for justice. We commit to centering Black Latinx voices, experience, and leadership.

To our Black brothers and sisters, we see you. We love you. Your lives matter.

With love,

Mujeres Unidas y Activas

(Posted http://mujeresunidas.net, July 15, 2016)

Skin

Gloria Amescua

(after *Synecdoche*, 1998, a painting by Kim Byron)
nameless paint chips

pale, palest, darkest
dark, paler, darker
...so many shades in between
in no particular order
varied as genes

beige coon chink meskins murder
    'rab hate purity nigger homie crime
wop brown kike coconut status lies
    mestizaje cheat jailbird greaser white
privilege mung blame cream oreo poverty
    walls slaughter redskin jap profile war
cracker beaner bindi ruddy honky race
    yellow hate wetback hangings power
boss hymie hoodies tan money guns
    redneck hate castes boats muslim loner
slavery hate chocolate freedom grief
    towel-head coffee suspect drugs hate
terrorist shame black stigma hate fear

flesh—
the husk we shed at death

(2016)

When They ... (Sanction This Violence)

MARIA TERESA "MARIPOSA" FERNANDEZ

you will hear
ritmos de resistencia
rattle in the bones

bones in all the bodies
con los ritmos de mis negritas y negritos
so black and beautiful / all shades of earth

earth mother / mother earth deeper than
any pride you could ever know/ que orgullo
fragile bodies of water

water as in blood /sangre
as in bloodlines/ salt /como lagrimas / plasma chains as fragile
as the screams your covered over ears could not hear/ fragile as
your babies' breath

breath breathing
in all the life of this contaminated planet
struggling to survive
breath breathing / in all the damn privileges/space/precious
resources

survive / survive/ survive this dark age / survive this truth /
survive this lie / survive this moment

survive these scenes on your tv screens / of the United States of
America / a car tears through black, brown, white bodies
standing against hate / violence on all sides? / oh someone's
little darling / white hooded toddler as plain as sesame street /
little white hood to match little white robe sewn by white-

mutha hands / your eyes are not deceiving you / it is 2017 / and hands / and twisted twisted twisted

imaginations / are quite creative and politicians quite cleaver / no this is not a figment of your imagination / this white supremacist nation / racist ideation // climate denier suicidal tendencies whipping in hurricane force winds / so you think you can tell heaven from hell? / turning up legacies

legacies traced back to bodies / swingin / negritas y negritos
in chains reflected in the whites our eyes as we watch the out of order news / in our
mass incarceration / nation and a NEW season of police killings / and brute force

force us to have the talk AGAIN where we tell our children / best not to speak at all
survive the encounter // ask: am I being detained officer? Am I free to go? am I being detained officer? Am I free to go? / Hands up // don't shoot // hands up / don't shoot racista

racista racista racista HERE WE GO RACISTA
white lights bright lights
on the nycha street corner /shine bright on the corner bodega of my block full of cops
shine bright on the hype white lights bright lights on the wall not talle enuf / for you cabrón / mister obscence killer of dreams

when they sanction this violence
you will hear todos los ritmos de resistencia
rattle in all the bones

bones of our ancestors
and it will be your worst fuckin nightmare
and you will scream
and then you will be awake.

(2017)

LGBTQ Struggles for Human Rights
(Lesbian, gay, bisexual, transgendered and queer)

Queer

NANCY LORENZA GREEN

Queer
as in different
as in one who stands out
in a unique way

Queer
as in one who makes others uncomfortable
as in one who threatens the established norms

Queer
as in rebel
as in one who doesn't mind being in your face
especially when you use terms like
strange, unusual, out of alignment, or sexual deviant

Queer
as in I love myself for who I am
as I love who you are in the most unique queer way
as in I feel empowered to decide my life
and to choose a partner I can respect
for being queer, two-spirited,
lesbian, gay, bisexual, transgender, queer-friendly

(First published in *Sinister Wisdom: A Multicultural Lesbian Literary and Art Journal*, "Out Latina Lesbians," Special Issue. Eds. Nivea Castro and Geny Cabral, 2015.)

An estimated 1.4 million—or 4.3 percent—of Latinx adults living in the United States identify as lesbian, gay, bisexual, or transgender (LGBT) according to a 2010 report based on U.S. Census data.*

Lesbian, gay, bisexual, and transgender, or LGBT women are among the most at risk of poverty. In the U.S., Latinas in same-sex couples are two times more likely to be poor than white women in same-sex couples. **

* The Williams Institute, UCLA School of Law, Report. Estimated 1.4 Million Latino/a Adults in the U.S. Identify as LGBT," 2013.

** Center for American Progress, Press Release. "LGBT Women Are Among Most at Risk of Poverty in America," 2015.

Why I interrupted Obama

JENNICET GUTIÉRREZ

Pride celebrations of the LGBTQ community are taking place throughout the nation. The community takes great pride in celebrating our diversity, and the progress we have made throughout the years. However, for the immigrant LGBTQ community progress has not been fully realized because of the continuous discrimination and violence we face in our daily lives.

I was fortunate to be invited to the White House to listen to President Obama's speech recognizing the LGBTQ community and the progress being made. But while he spoke of 'trans women of color being targeted,' his administration holds LGBTQ and trans immigrants in detention. I spoke out because our issues and struggles can no longer be ignored.

Immigrant trans women are twelve times more likely to face discrimination because of our gender identity. If we add our immigration status to the equation, the discrimination increases. Transgender immigrants make up one out of every 500 people in detention, but we account for one out of five confirmed sexual abuse cases in ICE Immigration and Customs Enforcement) custody.

The violence my trans sisters face in detention centers is one of torture and abuse. The torture and abuse come from ICE officials and other detainees in these detention centers. I have spoken with my trans immigrant sisters who were recently released from detention centers. With a lot of emotional pain and heavy tears in their eyes, they opened up about the horrendous treatment they all experienced. Often seeking asylum to escape threats of violence because of their gender identity and sexuality, this is how they're greeted in this country. At times misgendered, exposed to assault, and put in detention centers with men.

Last night I spoke out to demand respect and acknowledgement of our gender expression and the release of the estimated seventy-five transgender immigrants in detention right now. There is no pride in how LGBTQ immigrants are treated in this country, and there can be no celebration with an administration that has the ability to keep us detained and in danger or release us to freedom.

It is heartbreaking to see how raising these issues were received by the president and by those in attendance. In the tradition of how Pride started, I interrupted his speech because it is time for our issues and struggles to be heard. I stood for what is right. Instead of silencing our voices, President Obama can also stand and do the right thing for our immigrant LGBTQ community.

(First published in www.washingtonblade.com, 2015.)

Fairy Dust

LILLIANA VALENZUELA

She looked at me, nervously
her eyes zigzagging
she felt herself seen
questioned, perhaps
a woman-protest-sign
between two bathrooms
at the airport.

No sign, no words,
just her presence
on a Thursday morning
in Charlotte, North Carolina.
Her frilly white dress
her white tights and
white platform heels
fairy white hair
and lacey dark eyebrows
framing her mustache
and beard.
A person. A sign. A stand.
An interrogation.

She stood quietly, maybe
waiting to use the restroom.
Not knowing which
not knowing how
calling our attention
declaring her right to exist.

(2017)

PART 3.

FIGHT FOR REPRODUCTIVE JUSTICE!

One night Gloria Anzaldúa saw a vision of the Virgen de Guadalupe in her beloved cypress tree. "La Aparición" interprets this vision as a giant vulva rising out of the legs of the tree to signal this virgin's resonances with Pachamama or Mother Nature, and to center women's sexual and erotic pleasure.

Claudia Sofia Garriga López

La Aparición

Claudia Sofia Garriga López

Black feminists coined the term "reproductive justice" in 1994 to express the belief that women have the right to decide whether, when, and how to have and parent children. The term included the idea that women who choose to parent should be able to raise their children in a safe and healthy environment. Reproductive justice merges the reproductive rights and social justice struggles.

Loretta Ross and Rickie Solinger, *Reproductive Justice: An Introduction (Reproductive Justice: A New Vision for the 21st Century)* 1st Edition (Oakland: University of California Press, 2017)

Latina/o/xs[1] and Reproductive Justice in the United States

Jessica González-Rojas

In the fall of 2017, a minor referred to as "Jane Doe" stood before a Texas judge seeking to obtain a judicial waiver for an abortion. Jane, a 17-year old Latina, came to the United States without documents and unaccompanied by her parents. She learned that she was pregnant while held in detention at a children's shelter run by the U.S. Department of Health and Human Services' Office of Refugee Resettlement (ORR). Jane decided that she was not ready to become a parent and sought an abortion. She secured funding for the procedure, but the Trump administration intervened and refused to allow her to leave the facility to receive the medical care that she required.

Jane and her lawyers from the American Civil Liberties Union (ACLU) navigated a ping-pong of court decisions to fight for the care she needed. Although the Texas judge authorized Jane to receive the abortion, ORR ordered her to go to a religiously affiliated "Crisis Pregnancy Center" instead; there she received biased and medically inaccurate information attempting to force her to continue her pregnancy. In a statement released by the ACLU, Jane stated:

> "While the government provides for most of my needs at the shelter, they have not allowed me to leave to get an abortion. Instead, they made me see a doctor that tried to convince me not to abort and to look at sonograms. People I don't even know are trying to make me change my mind. I made my decision and that is between me and God. Through all of this, I have never changed my mind....

---

1. Conscious of the importance of gender equality in the production of educational materials in the English language, the National Latina Institute for Reproductive Health utilizes gender-neutral terms. "Latinx" is a term that challenges the gender binary in the Spanish language and embraces the diversity of genders that often are actively erased from space. Note that the term Latinx is not used when citing statistics.

It has been very difficult to wait in the shelter for news that the judges in Washington, D.C. have given me permission to proceed with my decision. I am grateful for this, and I ask that the government accept it. Please stop delaying my decision any longer."[2]

After a month of delays, numerous court cases, and appeals, Jane Doe finally obtained the abortion she needed on October 25, 2017.

REPRODUCTIVE JUSTICE

Jane's story is representative of the reproductive injustices that Latina/o/xs in the United States face every day. Her story is about reproductive rights, but also about immigration status and a young woman's autonomy. It highlights how a woman's ability and right to make decisions about her body and reproduction are limited by poverty, race, ethnicity, immigration status, age, and other social factors and institutional systems.

The National Latina Institute for Reproductive Health is dedicated to building Latina power to guarantee the fundamental human right to reproductive health, dignity, and justice. We advance a vision for reproductive justice and human rights that includes the ability to decide if and when to have children, build families, and parent children with dignity, and freedom from immigration policies that disregard our humanity.

Reproductive justice is a framework and approach to organizing for social change that centers the needs, voices, and leadership of those who are marginalized/oppressed, including women of color, low-income people, LGBTQ people, young parents, and immigrants, understanding that a person's identities determines access to power and resources. Reproductive justice seeks to identify, name, and dismantle these systems of oppression and build a just world where all people can thrive.

---

2. American Civil Liberties Union, "After A Month of Obstruction by the Trump Administration, Jane Doe Gets Her Abortion," (American Civil Liberties Union, October 25, 2017) https://www.aclu.org/news/after-month-obstruction-trump-administration-jane-doe-gets-her-abortion

Latinx Reproductive Health Care

Advancing a vision for reproductive justice is critical. One in five Latinas live in poverty, with a whopping 41 percent of Latina-headed households below the federal poverty level.[3] This reality results in alarming health consequences. Latinas experience disproportionately high rates of unintended pregnancy,[4] sexually transmitted infections including HIV,[5] diabetes,[6] asthma,[7] and other negative health outcomes. They face preventable health conditions and are among the most likely to suffer and die from cervical cancer, an almost entirely preventable and treatable disease.[8] Latinas are diagnosed with cervical cancer at nearly twice the rate of non-Latina white women.[9]

Multiple factors contribute to these disturbing statistics including less access to affordable preventive services, less exposure to comprehensive sexuality education, less contraceptive education and use, and higher rates of contraceptive failure. Historically, the high cost of contraception has made it difficult for Latinxs to access birth control; Latinas experience unintended pregnancy at twice the rate of

---

3. National Women's Law Center, "National Snapshot: Poverty Among Women and Families, 2015" (National Women's Law Center, September 2016), https://nwlc.org/wp-content/uploads/2016/09/Poverty-Snapshot-Fact sheet-2016.pdf

4. Susan A. Cohen, "Abortion and Women of Color: The Bigger Picture," Guttmacher Policy Review 11 no. 3 (Summer 2008), http://www.guttmacher.org/pubs/gpr/11/3/gpr110302.pdf.

5. Centers for Disease Control and Prevention, "HIV/AIDS: HIV Among Latinos," last modified Jan. 23, 2014, http://www.cdc.gov/hiv/risk/ra cialethnic/hispaniclatinos/facts/index.html.

6. Office of Minority Health, "Diabetes and Hispanic Americans" US Department of Health and Human Services, last modified June 13, 2014, http://minorityhealth.hhs.gov/omh/browse.aspx?lvl=4&lvlID=63.

7. Office of Minority Health, "Asthma and Hispanic Americans," US Department of Health and Human Services, last modified Sept. 23, 2014, http://minorityhealth. hhs.gov/omh/browse.aspx?lvl=4&lvlID=60.

8. Centers for Disease Control and Prevention, "Gynecologic Cancers: Cervical Cancer Rates by Race and Ethnicity," last modified Aug. 27, 2014, http://www.cdc.gov/cancer/cervical/statistics/race.htm.

9. Latinas contract cervical cancer at 1.6 times the rate of white women. US Department of Health and Human Services, "The Affordable Care Act and Latinos," last modified Nov. 5, 2014, http://www.hhs.gov/healthcare/ facts/factsheets/2012/04/aca-and-latinos04102012a.html.

their white peers.[10] Evidence shows that lesbian, gay, and bisexual youth may experience unintended pregnancies at even higher rates than their heterosexual peers suggesting that LGBTQ Latinx youth also need access to resources and tools, contraception, and comprehensive sexuality education[11] to achieve positive health outcomes.

People of color and low-income people in the U.S. have long struggled to obtain the same health care, and exercise the same constitutionally protected reproductive rights as their white and higher-income counterparts. While the Supreme Court recognized a constitutional right to abortion in 1973, the promise of self-determination and reproductive equity has remained out of reach for people of color and low-income people due in large part to the Hyde Amendment, which bans federal funding for abortion coverage through Medicaid and has promulgated look-alike policies that deny insurance coverage for abortion to many others.

Latinxs' access to abortion care remains under attack and disparities persist. Restrictions on public insurance coverage for abortion care have a harmful impact on Latinx who are more likely to be enrolled in public insurance programs. In fact, in 2012, 29 percent of Latino adults and children were enrolled in Medicaid.[12] Bans on insurance coverage for abortion put Latinxs and their families in untenable economic situations. For those who qualify and enroll in Medicaid, the cost of ending a pregnancy may force a choice between paying for rent or groceries, or paying for medical care.

Latinxs are uninsured/underinsured at higher rates than any other racial or ethnic group. Lesbian, gay, bisexual, transgender, and queer (LGBTQ) Latinxs face added healthcare discrimination, and are less likely to have access to insurance due to employment discrimination and lack of relationship recognition for partners and dependents. In 2016, 24.8 percent of Latinos remained uninsured, compared to only

---

10. Susan A. Cohen, "Abortion and Women of Color."

11. Lisa L. Lindley & Katrina M. Walsemann, Sexual Orientation and Risk of Pregnancy Among New York City High-School Students, 105 American Journal of Public Health 1379 (2015).

12. Kaiser Commission on Key Facts, Health Coverage for the Hispanic Population Today and Under the Affordable Care Act, (Kaiser Family Foundation, April 2013): 3, http://kff.org/disparities-policy/report/health-coverage-for-the-hispanic-population-today-and-under-the-affordable-care-act/.

8.7 percent for their white counterparts.[13] Despite passage of the Affordable Care Act (ACA), Latinxs continued to face barriers in accessing affordable insurance coverage, and many Latinxs were completely ineligible for ACA because of immigration status.

A PATH FORWARD

Reproductive justice is people working for social change, for a broad and intersecting set of issues, and on behalf of many communities and viewpoints. It values the multiple identities of our diverse communities; centers the voices of all Latinxs; promotes new and relevant leadership from the local, state and national levels and recognizes the need to build power locally to influence and change national policies. Reproductive justice places our work within the broader social justice movement strengthened by the development of coalitions and partnerships. This vision harnesses collective action to advocate for the needs of our communities so that we can someday see a world where all Latinxs, immigrants, people of color, women, femmes, LGBTQ folks, people with disabilities and those who earn low-incomes can thrive with full dignity and self-determination.

Reproductive justice will be attained when all people have the economic, social, and political power and means to make decisions about their bodies, sexuality, health, and family. It affirms that all people—regardless of where they live, how much they earn or their immigration status—should have access to the full range of reproductive health care, including abortion care, and be able to create and raise families in environments safe from state-sanctioned violence and militarization.

For the National Latina Institute for Reproductive Health and our *poderosas* (our powerful activists throughout the country), reproductive justice is a *movement*. It is our determination to advance and protect all people's fundamental human right to *salud, dignidad y justicia*—health, dignity and justice.

(2017)

---

13. Michelle M. Dotty, and Sara R. Collins, "Millions more Latino Adults Insured under the Affordable Care Act," The Commonwealth Fund, (January 19, 2017).

No Other Choice: A Comment on Latinas and Abortion Access on the 40th Anniversary of the Death of Rosie Jiménez

Elena R. Gutiérrez

October 3, 2017 was the Fortieth Anniversary of the death of Rosaura (Rosie) Jiménez, the first known person to die after an illegal abortion following the passage of the Hyde Amendment in 1976. Introduced three years after Roe v. Wade, which legalized abortion in the United States, Hyde bars the use of federal monies for abortion services except in life-threatening cases or pregnancies resulting from incest or rape. Although there is some variation in different states, Hyde essentially makes abortion legally available but financially inaccessible to those of low-income, whom are predominantly people of color and immigrants.[1]

The daughter of migrant farm-workers and one of twelve children, Rosie was a single-mother attending college in McAllen, Texas in 1977. Just six months away from earning a teaching credential from Pan American University, Rosie learned she was pregnant. Unable to afford the nearby clinic because it no longer accepted Medicaid due to Hyde's implementation, she traveled to an illegal abortionist who used unsterilized instruments during the procedure. Rosie died a few days later from a resulting infection, with a $700 scholarship check in her purse. Although this money could have been used to pay for a legal medical abortion, she'd decided to use it to complete her college education and move closer to her goal of becoming a special education teacher. Her belief that this was the best, and perhaps only, way to support her existing family poignantly underscores how empty the promise of "choice" is for many women in

---

1. Anonymous. "A Young Latina's Reflection on Choice." California Latinas for Reproductive Justice. Jan 2013. http://www.californialatinas.org/a-young-latinas-reflection-on-choice.

the United States.[2] It may also explain why Jiménez' legacy inspires so many individuals and organizations dedicated to repealing Hyde.

Despite consistent and growing efforts to dismantle Hyde over the past forty years, the amendment remains an obstacle to abortion access.[3] Recently published research and commentaries report that financial barriers remain a common and growing problem for Latinas in the United States.[4] One study predicted that more individuals than ever since the legalization of abortion would find themselves in circumstances similar to those faced by Rosie four decades ago.[5] This is even more true for Latinas, who have abortions at disproportionate rates despite the facts that more Latinas (37 percent) are uninsured than women of any other racial or ethnic group, over a quarter of Latinas live in poverty[6] and in areas with dwindling access to reproductive health services. One study estimated that between 17-20 percent of those in the United States who have abortions are

---

2. Ellen Frankfort, and Francis Kissling. *ROSIE: The Investigation of a Wrongful Death* (Doubleday, 1979).

3. "Research brief: The Impact of Medicaid Coverage Restrictions on Abortion." *Ibis Reproductive Health.* ND. Retrieved from https://ibisreproductivehealth.org/sites/default/files/files/publications/Research BriefImpactofMedicaidRestrictions.pdf.

4. For example: "Strong Families, Still Wading: Forty Years of Resistance, Resilience and Reclamation in Communities of Color." *Still Wading 2013.* ND. Retrieved from www.reproductivejusticeblog.org; Anonymous. "A Young Latina's Reflection on Choice." *California Latinas for Reproductive Justice.* Jan 2013. Retrieved from http://www. californialatinas.org/a-young-latinas-reflection-on-choice; "Latino Attitudes on Abortion: Roe v Wade 40 Years Later." *Latino World Media.* 2013. Retrieved from www.hispanicallyspeakingnews.com/latino-daily-news/details.

5. The Guttmacher Institute reported that during 2011 and 2012 more abortion restrictions were enacted in US states than in any other previous years. 2011 marked a record high, with 92 pieces of legislation being passed throughout the country. "2012 Saw Second-Highest Number of Abortion Restrictions Ever." *Guttmacher Institute.* 2013. Retrieved from https:// www.guttmacher.org/article/2013/01/2012-saw-second-highest-number-abortion-restrictions-ever.

6. Hope Gilette. "Cervical Cancer Awareness: Latinas at Greater Risk, 'Third Most Likely Group to Die of the Disease." Huffington Post. Jan 14, 2013. Retrieved from http://www.huffingtonpost.com/2013/01/14/latinas-at-greater-risk-for-cervical-cancer_n_2472472.html.

Latina.[7] For immigrants, who have little financial and social assistance and who may fear language barriers, racism or deportation, the circumstances are even more challenging.

Although research findings reflect that Latinas across the social spectrum have abortions, they also show that many do so because the circumstances of their lives simply offer <u>no other choice</u>. Thus, what is popularly perceived as open access to abortion in the United States is hardly the reality for most Latinas. As one "Anonymous- Reproductive Justice Advocate" notes: "The legality of Roe v. Wade does not reflect our country's culture where sex education is often-times limited to abstinence-only, access to birth control and abortion services is disproportionate, and interactions perpetuate slut-bashing where sexually-active youth are labeled as 'too sexual.'"[8]

While the author's anonymity signals how much further we must go in creating social safety for the one in three women in the United States who have abortions, the statement reinforces the need for broadening our understanding of abortion politics beyond legal access to consider the political context and economic circumstances within which individuals make reproductive decisions. As reproductive justice advocates have argued for decades, it is only from this perspective that we can speak about the significance of Roe v. Wade for Latinas.[9]

Recent research also reflects growing support for abortion in Latino communities. More generally, rather than being staunchly against it, a majority of Latinos hold compassionate views about abortion.[10] In one poll of Latina voters, 82% stated their belief that

7. "Latinas and Abortion Access: Issue Brief." *National Latina Institute for Reproductive Health.* 2004. Retrieved from latinainstitute.org/sites/default/files/publications/AbortionIssueBrief.pdf.

8. Anonymous. "A Young Latina's Reflection on Choice." *California Latinas for Reproductive Justice.* Jan 2013. Retrieved from http://www.californialatinas.org/a-young-latinas-reflection-on-choice.

9. Jael Silliman, Marlene Gerber Fried, Loretta Ross, Elena R. Gutierrez. *Undivided Rights: Women of Color Organize for Reproductive Justice.* (Cambridge MA: South End Press, 2004).

10. "Latino Abortion Attitude Polling" *National Latina Institute for Reproductive Health.* 2011. Retrieved from http://latina institute.org/publications/Poll-Latino-Voters-Hold-Compassionate-Views-on-Abortion

"women should make their own decisions" regarding abortion.[11] A separate study found that the majority of Latinas support repealing the Hyde Amendment.[12]

Another development since Rosie's death is the increased visibility of Latinas at the forefront of reproductive health, justice and rights organizing and advocacy. By working for policy change, providing health services and educating and mobilizing communities, practitioners, advocates and organizers realize the vision of a developing a reproductive justice movement that promotes an intersectional understanding of the many factors that shape someone's sexual and reproductive lives.[13] The Colorado Organization for Latina Opportunity and Reproductive Rights (COLOR), explains that:

> Reproductive justice affirms that a person has the right and should have the ability: (1) to decide when to become a parent, (2) to decide to not become a parent and (3) to raise their children in a safe and healthy environment... Going beyond abortion, reproductive justice recognizes the right to have a child, the right not to have a child, the right to parent the children we have with dignity, the right to control our birthing options, the right to choose our sexual partners, and the right to control our own gender.[14]

Thus, from a reproductive justice framework, while access to pregnancy termination through legal abortion is important, that alone is insufficient. Reproductive justice demands that in addition to

---

11. "Latino/a Voters' Views on Abortion." *PerryUndem Research/ Communication.* 2016. Retrieved from http://latinainstitute.org/sites/ default/les/NLIRH%20Public%20Survey%20Report_Final.pdf

12. "Battleground Polling on Repealing the Hyde Amendment." *Heart Research Associates.* 2016. Retrieved from: http: allaboveall.org/wp/wp-content/uploads/2016/09/AllAbove-All_Hart_Battleground-Poll-2016-Memo.pdf

13. It is not that this is a new occurrence—Latinas have taken care of their bodies and advocated for reproductive health issues, including pregnancy termination, for longer than Roe v. Wade has been in existence. See Gutierrez, "We Will No Longer be Silent or Invisible" in Undivided Rights: Women of Color Organize for Reproductive Justice (2nd edition, Haymarket Press, 2017)

14. "Reproductive Justice." *Colorado Organization for Latina Opportunity and Reproductive Rights.* ND. Retrieved from http:// www.colorlatina.org/ content/reproductive-justice

increased access to abortion services, we must also create a society that supports all persons having the freedom, rights and resources to not have a child, or to have as many as they want. Moreover, all people should have the right to parent the children they have with full access to the social resources necessary to raise them in safe and healthy environments, without fear of violence from individuals or institutions, or intervention by the government. This is particularly true given the long history of birth control testing, medical experimentation, sterilization abuse, and other forms of reproductive coercion that various Latinx communities have experienced throughout their interaction with Western cultures.

Thus, in addition to safe, affordable, and culturally proficient health care, we must make assistive reproductive technologies available, fund education, invest in health care reform for all, ensure safe and nutritious food security, and prioritize family reunification. That each of these options be guaranteed be for all people regardless of race, class, gender, sexuality, physical ability, citizenship or any other social difference, is fundamental to creating true reproductive justice for Latinxs, their families and communities.

If you would like to learn more about Latinxs and abortion, reproductive justice or efforts to end the Hyde Amendment:

1. Find out about the abortion laws in your state, and the existence of an abortion fund (check out the National Network of Abortion Funds (NNAF) http://www.fundabortionnow.org/). They will also be able to assist someone in your area with various resources and support. (NNAF).

2. See the many bi-lingual fact sheets and policy analyses offered by the National Latina Institute for Reproductive Health at: www.latinainstitute.org/issues/abortion-access, or others listed in the footnotes.

3. Find out if there is a reproductive justice organization in your state. Volunteer, recommend, donate, and keep connected to the issues. If you can't find one, think about starting one!

4. The Repeal Hyde Art Project offers an easy way to begin organizing in your community: http://www.repealhydeartproject.org/hyde-amendment/. Spreading the word and educating others about Hyde and abortion access is a meaningful contribution and helps reduce stigma.

5. To learn more about reproductive justice in general, the Reproductive Justice Virtual Library, with online access to over 200 articles, reports and document, is a good place to start: https://www.law.berkeley.edu/research/center-on-reproductive-rights-and-justice/crrj-reproductive-justice-virtual-library/.

(Small portions of this essay were previously published in *Mujeres Talk* blog, "Latinas and Roe v. Wade," Jan. 21, 2013. https://library.osu.edu/blogs/mujerestalk/2013/01/21/latinas-and-roe-v-wade/)

PART 4.

SEXUAL ASSAULT, RAPE & STATE VIOLENCE

1 IN 3

LATINAS HAVE
EXPERIENCED
DOMESTIC VIOLENCE

National Latin@ Network
www.nationallatinonetwork.org/

Yes All Women

EMILY PÉREZ

on a crowded train and yes
all women and maybe
it was not okay
to share upon the sudden
thought this awful thing
that popped to mind
when a friend mentioned
that she in an alley
like something else that just
will happen that I like them
had been and I'm all grown
and they are girls already
trodden gently down
trodden I said it because
they've heard it and it will seem
so far away and then one day
you are and it's like *oh*
this is the way
it's what's supposed
to come this time this day
one day one man can make
you a number on a graph
a number in a grim brochure

one man says he ensures his daughters
are protected by not telling them
this day awaits instead
it comes
like a bubble burst
no use get used
get used
to it
it comes
it comes it comes

(2017)

Hashtag #MeToo

IRIS MORALES

The history of sexual assault and rape in the Americas begins with the enslavement of African and Indigenous people. Picture black and native women running, terrified, screaming with fear, crying, and pleading for their lives. Women fought and resisted in every way they could, even joining slave uprisings and rebellions. After slavery ended, violence and murder continued to terrorize the entire black population, and African American women led campaigns against all forms of violence, including rape. Generations of black and brown women continued to organize against sexual violence, and this demand remains a cornerstone of the movement for women's rights today.

In 2006, Tarana Burke, an African American activist, founded Just Be Inc., an organization focused on the health and well being of young women of color dedicated to helping sexual assault victims. Ms. Burke began to use the phrase "Me too" on the MySpace social network as part of a grassroots effort to promote "empowerment through empathy" among women of color. This "Me too" campaign intended to support sexual violence survivors, especially women in low-income communities where rape crisis centers did not exist. It was a way to connect survivors, and encourage sisterhood and healing.

More than ten years later in October 2017, in the midst of the sexual abuse scandal against Hollywood mogul Harvey Weinstein, the actress Alyssa Milano posted a note on Twitter that read, "Suggested by a friend: If all the women who have been sexually harassed or assaulted wrote "Me too" as a status, we might give people a sense of the magnitude of the problem." She asked people to reply "me too" to her tweet. To her surprise, tens of thousands of people replied describing personal experiences of sexual assault. The hashtag #MeToo became a rallying point and exposed the pent up outrage that had few outlets to be heard.

Dozens of female actresses and celebrities, including Latinas, tweeted about their experiences with sexual predators in the film and entertainment industry. Their stories garnered widespread media headlines, and their personal revelations exposed sexual abuse that led to the downfall of many prominent and powerful men.

Although the mainstream media focused primarily on the accounts of celebrities, thousands of women from all walks of life across the world also responded to the #MeToo hashtag. Sexual violence was not a new or isolated problem. Women showed the prevalence of sexual assault in workplaces, schools, on the streets, inside government institutions, and throughout society. Women of color suffered the highest rates of sexual violence; they experience both racialized and sexualized attacks and rape, the legacy of slavery and racism previously discussed.

#MeToo brought to the forefront the pervasiveness of sexual assault in all industries and sectors. It also highlighted the situation of women with few or no economic options, especially low-income and undocumented women of color disproportionately in the ranks of the poor and working class who are particularly vulnerable targets. Reporting any assault, even rape, is often unthinkable because too much is at risk—losing a job that feeds the entire family or even being deported from the country. The Alianza Nacional de Campesinas made this point in a letter of solidarity to the #MeToo movement. Representing approximately 700,000 farmworker women and farmworker families, their statement circulated widely on the Internet and aided in expanding the discussion about the scope of the problem.

The hashtag #MeToo created an opening for a public discussion. It was a catalyst that inspired millions of women and men to break their silence and speak out about the universality and systemic character of sexual violence and other injustices against women. The challenge ahead is to translate the heightened awareness into collective activism and organizing to achieve the wide-ranging societal changes that are needed.

(2018)

110

Unoriginal Danger

DOMINIQUE SALAS

During commercial breaks, Abuelita retold a story
I was already told, not by her, but by myself,
in a way. But really, she had told me the story
before. In her rural town outside of Chihuahua, her tía
was reassigned from male hands to male hands to
dirt. La violaron; literally, men had violated her.
For this, her wrists were tied and strung behind a cart
so that when her father cracked the whips against the horses'
rear, her body would gallop bloody behind the cart. In all
my Americanized pocha-ness, her story is an argument
that has helped me now. La violaron: he violated her. His
body acted in conflict with the principle of her
personhood. El la violó. Her, the person; Her, the idea; her,
in which the vacancies of flesh were taken as a request. Too simple
for me was it to say She was raped or She was a survivor. No,
la violaron por andando de puta. Andando de puta when
riding a horse like a man. Andando de puta when yelling,
¡Me vale madre! when told to cross my legs ¡Que se me ve
la cocina! Andando de puta winding on everyone's lap
at that party. Por andando de puta, me violaron. Nunca me he
gustado dicirlo pero, I found it's the principle of my body's matter.

(2017)

What Rape Culture Looks Like in the Latinx Community

RAQUEL REICHARD

That's a difficult comment to make when the U.S. sitting president, Donald Trump, won the election on a campaign that falsely demonized Latinxs, particularly Mexican immigrants, as rapists, but it's one we need to make if we are going to address the real issue.

Before we do that, however, it's crucial that I note that rape culture –a setting where rape is normalized and trivialized and where victims are blamed—is a worldwide problem that isn't exclusive to Latinxs or Latin America—far from it.

Violence and aggression pose threats to people everywhere. According to the United Nations, one in five women across the globe will be a victim of rape or attempted rape in her lifetime. In fact, women between the ages of 15 and 44 are more at risk of being sexually assault than having cancer or getting into a car accident. Among the ten countries with the highest incidence of rape are nations in Europe, the Americas, and Africa.

Let's be clear: the issue is rampant and international. As such, it is also a serious problem among the Latino community. A National Violence Against Women Survey found that 21.2 percent of Latina women have experienced sexual assault. As the number of Latinxs in the country continues to skyrocket, researchers believe that Latina rape and sexual assault survivors will also increase. It is believed that by the year 2050, <u>10.8 million</u> Latinas in the United States will be survivors of sexual violence.

Making this brutality worse is the ways in which our culture-- from music and television shows to education and quips—perpetuates rape. If we are going to combat this violence, which we must, we need to understand what it looks like. With that, here are 18 examples of rape culture in the Latino community.

1. The objectification and sexualization of Latinas in media, from advertisements and films to newscasts and memes.

2. Spanish-language hit songs about men "seducing and abusing" women and telling them not to "refuse" it, tunes like Alexis Y Fido's "A Ti Te Encanta" ("You Love It").

3. Glamourizing and romanticizing Latin American drug lords who rape women (think every drug-cartel film and show, including the Netflix hit "Narcos").

4. Mexican TV host Tania Reza being sexually harassed on-air, forced to call the attack a hoax, and then losing her job.

5. Praising and defending alleged rapists because they're celebrities, like actor-TV host Mario Lopez, who was accused of date raping women in 1991 and 1993. According to Dustin Diamond, who worked with Lopez on "Saved By The Bell," NBC paid one of the women $50,000 to stay quiet about the rape.

6. Latina teen Cherice Moralez committing suicide after a judge sentenced the 50-year-old man who raped her to just 30 days in jail because the girl, who was curvy, looked "older than her chronological age."

7. Children, like a 10-year-old girl from Paraguay, being forced to carry pregnancies resulted from rape to term.

8. Street harassment making women feel less safe then men while walking around at night, and Latinas experiencing this cat-calling, touching and stalking earlier than all other racial and ethnic groups in the country.

9. Latina teens dropping out of school to avoid being sexually harassed instead of schools fighting to end the violence.

10. Seventy-seven percent of Latinas saying that sexual harassment is a major problem in the workplace.

11. Religious Latinx parents telling their daughters not to make men sin by showing too much skin or wearing form-fitting clothes.

12. Latinas being taught to prevent rape and sexual assault instead of men being told not to rape.

13. Victim-blaming by saying women who dress provocatively, flirt, or dare to drink at night are asking to be raped.

14. Latinas being raised to believe that sex is a marital obligation, and married Latinas being the least likely to define marital rape as rape.

15. Central American girls and women crossing the Mexico-U.S. border taking birth control because <u>80 percent</u> of them will be raped.

16. Rape jokes about women and imprisoned men, and those who laugh and support them.

17. Latina hashtag results including mostly half-naked (or fully nude) Latinas.

18. Leading search engine results for "Latinas and rape" including porn site links like "Latina teen pussy rape porn," "hot forced Latinos sex," "Latina rape videos" and more.

While Latinxs aren't alone in maintaining rape culture, as this list shows, our community does perpetuate it, and only by understanding the different ways it manifests can we begin to challenge it.

(First published at Latina.com, 2015)

Bronx Lloronas

Nia Andino

I.

Girls
Bodies
Parks/Posters/ Bones
Bodies
Vans/Vigils/ Coins
Bodies
Mothers/Rivers/Bedrooms
Bodies
Caskets
Silence
Girls
Bodies

II.

photos of the girls have been released
and mami fears you left here thinking her voice knew nothing
but flames
she was not always a closed fist
she just learned to never be an open palm
Emily was supposed to come home from a juvenile program
Sierra might have run off with her boyfriend
maybe Ashley was sick of the Bronx and ditched her little sister
who the fuck knows?
but the photos of the girls have been released
and there is a market for selling girls here
a currency for the desperate

III.

mami's grief is eating again
I can see her insides join us at the table
we supper in silence
unless her mouth is flooded
anxious to find you
preparing whether to clutch the buried
or mourn the returned

IV.

cotton sheets and dry towels cannot mask the clocks ticking
the voices itching when bereaved carnations breathe
your photo is removed
sympathies have good intentions when they sing piled on the floor
there is crying inside.
                              it continues next door.
floors creak
with ghost girls
novenas
and sopping mops.
mami can't smell you anymore.
                              over the Fabuloso,
and the dirty water she carries to the parkway river

IV.

there is cottonmourn on the clothes mami picks from your closet
sometimes she will carry one thing of yours
to where the Lloronas congregate
and remember how their fire turned to too much water
how your delayed silence
was remorsefully granted
and how their daughter's names in bellywail
pain like birth again

(2016)

Ten Acts of State Violence
Latinas Encounter in the U.S.

RAQUEL REICHARD

Imagine a perpetrator of violence against women. Some people envision a hooded stranger hiding behind a bush while others, perhaps more familiar with the data on sexual assault, are picturing a relative or family friend. What doesn't usually come to mind is our government, but there is a long and ongoing history of U.S.-sanctioned efforts to control and violate our bodies, and it isn't exclusive to our reproductive abilities either.

From forced sterilizations to police killings, governmental and legal institutions execute policies and practices that repress, control and brutalize Latinas, among other women of color. Here are just ten examples of these acts of state violence.

1. FORCED STERILIZATION

In 1975, ten Mexican-American women filed a historic lawsuit after they were sterilized at a Los Angeles hospital, many without their informed consent. The case, Madrigal v. Quilligan, and the coercive sterilizations are spotlighted in "No Más Bebés," the documentary released in 2016. But they weren't alone. The film highlights the ways the United States has justified denying Latinas their bodily autonomy through coercive population control. The U.S. was practicing this form of "population control" in Puerto Rico dating back to the 1930s, performing the procedure on poor women who were not told they would become infertile, or they were informed in English, a language they did not understand. As recently as 2014, Latina inmates, along with other women prisoners of color, were coerced into sterilization in a California prison.

2. GUINEA PIGS FOR MEDICAL RESEARCH

Also in Puerto Rico, at least 1,500 women were used as guinea pigs for dangerous and unethical birth control trials in the mid-1950s. Previously, the drug had only been tested on rats, rabbits, and a small group of women in Massachusetts. But the largest trial run was on the island where women were given significantly higher doses than is used today. Three women in the trials died though no autopsies were conducted to determine if their deaths were linked to the drugs.

3. GASOLINE BATHS

In the early 20th century, the United States deloused Mexican housekeepers crossing the border each day by stripping and bathing them in toxic gasoline mixtures. Even more, the women were further violated and shamed as their naked bodies were photographed and shared. The deadly procedure went on for decades, even after a 17-year-old maid named Carmelita Torres started a protest attended by thousands of Mexican dissidents, including many women.

4. POLICE KILLINGS

Jessie Hernandez is one of countless unarmed teenagers of color whose lives were taken by police officers. The 17-year-old queer Latina from Denver was gunned down in 2015 by an officer who professed he did so in self-defense though an autopsy proved his claims false. She was murdered for driving a "suspicious vehicle."

5. MASS INCARCERATION

Latinas are among the fastest-growing prison populations. The number of women behind bars has been increasing since 1980 at almost twice the rate for men, and Latinas are 69 percent more likely to be jailed than white women. Many of these Latinas are locked up for nonviolent drug offenses.

6. HARSHER SENTENCES

Not only are Latinas more likely to be jailed than white women, but their sentences are often harsher too. On the state level, Latinas are 27.6 percent more likely to have a harsher sentence for a similar crime than their white counterparts. At the federal level, that number jumps to 47.6 percent.

7. US PATROL RAPES

Before embarking on their journey across the Mexico-U.S. border, Mexican and Central American women purchase birth control pills because they know that most women who make the trek are raped. However, it is less known that sometimes the perpetrator will be a representative of the U.S. government.

Between 2008 and 2014, more than twenty agents were accused of sexually assaulting, raping, and/or attempting to murder women crossing the border.

8. FAMILY DETENTION CENTER ABUSE

Even in family detention centers that house undocumented mothers and their children, women, and sometimes daughters, are subjected to abuse. Lawyers from Texas and Florida allege that their clients have experienced various forms of sexual abuse by guards from fondling to rape.

9. TRANS LATINA DETAINEES IMPRISONED WITH MEN

Undocumented transgender Latinas locked away in immigration detention centers are often detained alongside men, sometimes the very men who they are running away from. In the male population, these women are physically abused by guards and fellow inmates, sexually assaulted, and denied their identities, their names, and their truth.

10. FAMILIES TORN APART

Through mass incarceration and deportation, which disproportionately impact Latinas, families are ripped apart, oftentimes forcing children to enter into foster care where they are more likely to drop out of school, become overmedicated and engage in substance abuse. A 2013 study from the Chronicle of Social Change found that U.S.-born Latinxs are among the highest population in the foster care system.

(First published at Latina.com, 2016)

PART 5.

HERSTORIES REMEMBERED

My brown body is inherited

YSABEL Y. GONZALEZ

My brown body is inherited
    along with its jeweled head split
on a curb, blood lingering
    on pavement. It is the red
birthmark of a nation.
    I can't stop clawing at my mother's scar,
incessant legacy carved
    into my flesh like initials in oak.
The body threads violence to itself,
    welting wounds into offspring.
I discover the ache
    but not the why or how of it.
My body remembers history
    even when my brain is muddled,
as if one leg is shorter
    than the other, a hobble
reminding me
    this body's belonged
to others before me.
    It will see the same open casket
bear the same brown bruised face,
    twisted mouth open as if to say
it remembers resistance.

(Published in Tinderbox Journal, 2017)

On *Mate* & the Work

RUTH IRUPÉ SANABRIA

If you are true,
knife the phallic gourd.
Gut it & cure it.
Prepare it for drink.

If you are true,
allow me to choose
the yellow silicone
over the wild & humid *porongo*.
Allow me to drink from it.

Refugee exile
immigrant witch
estupida pendeja
puta bitch
dyke cunt
mala
madre, madre
mala
& with each hunt,
injured
even if
not caught.

How are you?

This *mate*, it's dish washable.
Bought it on Amazon.

This little grandmother
was ordered to pull down her paintings
because the Rabbi was offended
by her version of Eve: 9 months pregnant,
unbroken & reaching for another apple.

This little grandmother,
with the word *¡escuchá!*,
from prison, smuggles a poem to her daughter:
as is a seed,
as is a drop of water
we are bound
to a triumphant bloom,
& my joy is entangled
with that of my brothers & sisters;
& I couldn't abandon this love.

How to fill the cellular hunger for one's mother, if one's
mother is running?
What if one's mother is detained?
What if she is never the same, but one's hunger hasn't
changed?

This little grandmother
sent her daughter to Juarez with money
to be given specifically to a mother searching
for her daughter who had been kidnapped & murdered in
Juarez,
& specifically for the testimony she was giving
about her daughter kidnapped & murdered in Juarez
this mother was marked for death,
but she became 1000 mothers more.

Mates made of gourds steady palms.
Mates made of gourds remain composed.
Mates made of gourds hold the memory of touch.

This little grandmother
said the words plainly:
La triple jornada,
the triple shift:
at dawn the fork,
then the long obedience of the dollar
& after it is done,
and after dinner is done,
& the lover is loved, the dogs fed, &
as the children sleep
the work of justice and art begins
& her daughters understood.

Honey, syrup, or plain?
Boiled eggs or fried?
Two ponytails or one?
Breath, teeth, ears: check, check, check.
Lunch box, homework, sign & return,
dishwasher, laptop, phone,
car keys, house keys, chargers,
apples, waters, & I.D.s,
love you, love you, love you, listen
to your teachers, be kind, & remember,
listen isn't always the same as shut up, & remember
that the eye of the witness disarms the devil.

You can find this work, right here,
in the neighborhoods of your conscience.

Where can I find my eyes?

Silicone *mates* fall
& return upright & whole;
the fissure, a sorrow belonging
to the skull and its brain,
to the earth, her shells and her gourds.
Silicone *mates* travel unnoticed,
bent into themselves in the oppressive bulk
of crowded backpacks and hurried suitcases,
reshaping themselves like nothing.

What knot do you use to not fly away?
What is your mantra to keep your feet in line?
What is your anchor?

Never allow the water to boil.
Shake the *yerba* of its dust before pouring the first round.
Spit out your first sip.

Inspiration never comes over for *mate*.
Inspiration takes hours to get anything done.
Mostly, inspiration prefers to stay away
until you're almost done with what it is you called her for.

This little grandmother serves her husband *mate*:
Three sips at 4 o'clock every single day.
This little grandmother takes her *mate* alone,
after her husband has gone.
This little grandmother serves her husband *mate* in bed
before leaving to work.

This little grandmother is not bothered by you, little boy. You are fully integrated into her skin, her book, her breath, & she drinks maté in a sloppy American way: forgetting to shake the herb of its dust, forgetting to spit out her first sip, giving you a sip of it while it is still strong, throwing the silicone gourd in the dishwasher.

Not my daughter. What other offering, sky? Not my daughter.

Mind the kettle. Share the straw without fear.
If there is a sore on the lip or a cold in the lungs,
wipe the straw with a cloth & continue to share.

What are hands for? What are feet for? Heart? Voice?

We ask again & again.

Woke, mouth closed howling, industrious & on task.
To-do list scrolling down my back.

Thursday morning mother emptiness wakes me with a start, & drills itself into my left hip. My floors are gross, the wastebasket is growing a pool of blue mint, & I know you have some heart-balm. Friday night I'm pushing the cart through Shoprite; days show up & I'm unprepared, the walls are unfinished, there are nails sticking out, my roots are visible, my fingers are raw. It is Monday & the toilet is disgusting. It is Tuesday & I promise to pay when I am paid. Then, it is Wednesday, oils & bubbles in the water for the children, coconut for their hair. Thursday, I do not want to teach another unit on genocide. I am teaching another unit on genocide. Friday. Mother. But you are a bonfire, & when low, flame.

30 years ago: you sit at your handmade desk, working
but available to me for talk about some aspect of your life &
some aspect of mine.
Now, I sit in the car & I scroll to find your name.
But I swallow the ocean back. I am tidying up.

In this dream, I attend a conference of writers and professors.
You are dead. A woman reads from you.
She says you said that I said,
"use a word to use a word"
& this is how
by not abandoning this work, we don't abandon each other.

Once upon a time, a turtle took several decades to cross the
street,
to get itself up the side of the house,
through the back door, into the living room,
to stare at you and you were mortified.
How the fuck did this monstrosity of determination
make it in without me noticing?

(2017)

Excerpt From The Play
"Julia De Burgos: Child of Water"

CARMEN RIVERA

In 1942, the great Puerto Rican poet Julia de Burgos moved to Cuba, in an effort to escape the oppression of the Nationalist Movement in Puerto Rico. There is a story of her meeting the Poet Pablo Neruda at the Dominican writer Juan Bosch's house. This scene imagines that famous encounter.

SCENE

PLACE: JUAN BOSCH'S HOUSE - LA HAVANA, CUBA

Juan Bosch and Pablo Neruda enter.

PABLO: Bosch, she's amazing.

BOSCH: Didn't I tell you that?

PABLO: She sees; she hears something totally different than the rest of us.

BOSCH: The first time I heard her read poetry, I felt like a train hit me. She was simple, direct, and powerful.

PABLO: She reads with so much emotion – the poetry just flows out of her, you don't know it's a poem until she's half way through it. I don't think she even understands her talent.

BOSCH: Those are the best artists.

PABLO: She's the chosen one – she's been called to be the voice of Latin America.

Julia enters.

JULIA: Juan, the view from your terrace is so beautiful.

BOSCH: Thank you.

JULIA: The sounds of the waves are so peaceful and the moonlight …ah…I felt my skin burning in the moonlight. Despite all the tragedy in the world, being immersed in nature assures me that somehow, somewhere God exists.

BOSCH: Sorry to disappoint you, God doesn't exist.

PABLO: Be careful Bosch, God is in people's lives whether you like it or not.

BOSCH: I'm sure the communist party would like to know that Pablo Neruda believes in God.

PABLO: I didn't say I believed in God, I said God is important in people's lives or rather the idea of God.

JULIA: I'm not sure what God means – but there's definitely something…some force out there. I am certain it is not a misogynistic, patriarchal God that delights in punishing people.

BOSCH: Now you're talking about the church – It is one thing to have corrupt government oppress its own citizens, but it is another thing when the church supports those governments. The last concern for the church is the people they serve.

PABLO: I don't know why you are surprised by that Juan…the church has always been complicit with governments and armies and rich feudal families…that is the oldest alliance in the world.

JULIA: That's what happening in Puerto Rico – the government, the United States army, and "The Church" – they've all conspired against el pueblo Puertorriqueño. Nobody is fighting for the people…no one knows who to trust. Half the island supports the United States – we're colonized, we're divided – we're scared. That's unbelievable to me.

BOSCH: What does the church do?

JULIA: Nothing.

BOSCH: Doesn't that make you furious?

JULIA: Of course it does! I'm trying to do what I can...join organizations, write poems that document the oppression.

BOSCH: We need take a stand against the church. That's the only way the world can be a better place.

PABLO: We're writers Juan...we can take our stands with the only weapons we have – our thoughts, our stories, our feelings, our ideas, our pens...that's as powerful as any army...that's why you're here living in exile – that's why we're all living in exile –

BOSCH: That's not the point. I'm aware of what our weapons are. I repeat WE need to take an ACTIVE stand against the church – more people have been killed in the name of God than any other entity know to humanity.

JULIA: But you cannot blame God – God is not the church.

PABLO: My point!

BOSCH: People's belief in God created the church.

JULIA: No, powerful men, who want to own real estate and have political office created the church.

PABLO: I agree with Julia. God has nothing to do with the church.

BOSCH: You should know better Pablo...I'm disappointed in you.

PABLO: Being a communist doesn't mean you DON'T have faith!

JULIA: I agree with you. (*to Pablo*)

BOSCH: Julia, you cannot listen to Pablo...he feels nostalgic for Chile...I'm surprised nostalgia has softened you.

PABLO: Of course, I miss Chile...desperately, as I am sure you miss Santo Domingo and Julia misses Puerto Rico...But one has to have faith Juan.

BOSCH: I have faith; I have faith that we will have revolutions all over the world.

PABLO: Do you have faith in the spirit?

BOSCH: Don't tell me you do.

PABLO: I do. I pray often.

BOSCH: In a church?

PABLO: Sometimes, when there's nobody in it.

BOSCH: You don't want anyone to see you?

PABLO: I like the quiet. My prayers are clearer.

JULIA: I used to do that when I was at the university. It was so peaceful. (*reflective*) But now I even wonder if God hears prayers anymore.

PABLO: Faith Julia.

JULIA: Look at the world Pablo.... there's too much unhappiness. Look how Spain was destroyed by it's Civil War, and now the war in Europe...how many people have died...so many people are starving, suffering and nobody cares. It breaks my heart. God's not listening.

BOSCH: So you don't have faith?

JULIA: I do, but faith in humanity and what WE can do

BOSCH: I can live with that.

JULIA: I agree with you too Juan, to a certain extent – I don't think we should tell people not to believe in God…people are not going to stop believing in God because one person tells them NOT to…and I do believe in faith. I am a Pantheist – I believe in the immense power of nature - and we can tap into that power to change our life.

VOICE –OFF-STAGE: Sr. Bosch, telephone.

BOSCH: Excuse me for just a second. I'm expecting an important call from Santo Domingo. I have certain friends that oblige me with news from home.

Juan Bosch exits.

JULIA: I just want to tell you that I love your work…I memorized your TWENTY POEMS OF LOVE when I was a teenager.

PABLO: Thank you. Once your work is published and disseminated you never know who's going to be affected by it. I saw you read a poem last week. It was good.

JULIA: You saw me?

PABLO: At the university.

JULIA: Oh no – I read some new work – it was so rough.

PABLO: I was impressed with the one that began with Ay, ay, ay, mi grifa negra…I think that's it.

JULIA: "Ay, ay that I am grifa and pure black; kinkiness in my hair, kafir in my lips; and my flat nose Mozambique…" Then it goes…. Wait – I can't remember all of it – I'm just memorizing it now…ah yes…"Ay, Ay, Ay, my black race flees and with the white runs to become brown; to become the race of the future, fraternity of America!"

PABLO: It's very powerful – it stayed with me all night, but if I may...I have a comment.

JULIA: Of course I'll take criticism from Pablo Neruda.

PABLO: It's not criticism, but you read the poem with too much anger – the other night.

JULIA: Too much anger? One can never have enough anger.

PABLO: Anger doesn't belong in art.

JULIA: Of course it does. Everything belongs in art: anger, happiness, dreams, fear...

PABLO: That's not true.

JULIA: Pablo, people of African descent are treated horribly all over the world. It makes me so angry I have to write about it.

PABLO: That's good Julia, but you must transform the anger.

JULIA: I'm not sure what you mean.

PABLO: Art should come from love, not hate.

JULIA: I have to be honest with you, I don't agree. You write amazing political poems, didn't they come from anger.

PABLO: All of my poems come from love, even the political ones. Everything stems from love, love of self; love of land; love of culture; love of country; love of humanity...people who love do not oppress and support tyranny. If you want something, someone, some political system to change it's because of a love you have for a better world. Use the anger to write the poem, the anger comes from love – you should read it from love. Don't hold onto the anger. Anger will destroy you talent, it will make you bitter, it will destroy your soul. Don't ever let anger take over your heart.

JULIA: What if I'm surrounded by anger?

PABLO: Feel it, transform it and release it.

JULIA: That's not easy to do. It's almost impossible.

PABLO: You have no choice, that's what artists do. Are you working on anything now?

JULIA: Yes, I'm working on a collection, it may become two separate collections...I'm thinking of the titles CAMPOS or THE SEA AND YOU. But it's not ready at all.

PABLO: We always think it's never ready. Would you allow me to read the poems?

JULIA: Of course!! But they're rough.

PABLO: Julia...I have been very fortunate in my life for many reasons...but to witness the birth of a new artist is exciting and liberating. You're inspiring me to go home and write. I'd love to read your work.

JULIA: It'll be my pleasure. Thank you.

PABLO: If you permit me, I'd like to write an introduction to the work.

JULIA: You haven't even read the poems yet.

PABLO: I have faith in you Julia.

END OF SCENE.

Excerpt from *Julia de Burgos: Child of Water.*
(New York: Red Sugarcane Press, Inc., 2015)

Truth in the Negatives

Leticia Hernández-Linares

No hay fotos de Juana. No silver
plated impression from copper sheet,
no third dimension of eyebrow
and temple, emerging
from mercury and darkness.

Only pieces of her life in glass
cases as evidence--rusted
long scissors, a shawl she made, folded
into the smallest portion of itself.

To recreate her image, scavenge
rocks piled in her archive,
take them to Washington Square.
There among the spirits of poets
and bohemians and Italians, her dress--
a needle and thread trailing from unabashed seams,
will give her away.

Unconcerned with herself, she will
devise the offering into walls
for the encampments overflowing
from the same city that sectioned off
Natives and Mexicans into Gold Rush residue.

From less than one percent of landmarks
for women, to hot metal molded
into the name of an indigenous, African,
Spanish woman. That she owned land, raised
children alone, developed her ability to heal,

held steadfast to community, commemorated,
with her name on a plaque on a park bench. Fotos
de la cuidad de San Francisco that boasts
this landmark for a woman, stream digital now.

New monuments of ahistorical wealth
push into the sky anchored by structures
that resemble concrete coffins. Radiant city,
lit once by the chorus of other countries,
voices raised in pride and protest, and poetic

chronicles, reduced to the monotony of stacked
rectangles, metal cranes looming over a bench
in Washington Square where Juana Briones
sits with her solitary and fading memory, waiting.

(2016)

Despite Their Best Efforts

ROSE BEN-ONI

I was little more
than a bottle cap of whiskey
More than once
I was rebozo slung
over a sleepy mouthed junkie
for CK one
Mira the everyday people baby
Mira like opening fire with candy
Mira my matted hair so model
off duty
While others donned tiaras
worldpeace and bikinis
  I was sizing up
  cops and clergy
At seven I ravaged a nativity
sullied
the feet of baby jesus
so he wouldn't be so trusting
Mira if we are the world
  then I was a test of levees
  I saw to it all my dolls
  were potty-trained
  and waterboarded each on a gurney
At dawn when they came home
exhausted from the double shift
another follower dozed in an ice bath
with one less kidney

      I was but the cliffhanger
from the great flood
babbling to a broken city

The future
crumbling bricks
and overcrowding
I am the first language
    no one is speaking
Mira a different world
This is my blood and this
my body this time
you won't betray me
I am your kingdom come
the barricades
giving way mira even
the liquor stores are closing

(First published in *The American Poetry Review,* 2014.)

Women Organizing Women

Iris Morales

Women joined the New York chapter of the Young Lords in 1969 as the organization was being formed. We enlisted to fight poverty and racism; to end gender discrimination; to free Puerto Rico; and to improve our lives and those of our families. Our struggle was for justice against powerful economic interests and institutions, and we believed that the equality of women was inseparable from society's progress as a whole. With an enthusiastic sense of possibilities, we embraced "the revolution within the revolution." This phrase, from a speech delivered by Fidel Castro in 1966, had credited Cuban women with furthering the revolutionary process of that nation. The women in the Young Lords pursued a similar idea, a story within a story that is barely known.

The women in the Young Lords were rebels, passionate about social justice, and young—most of us were between sixteen and twenty-six years old. At the high point, approximately one-third of the members of the Young Lords were women. We were primarily Puerto Ricans, also African Americans, Cubans, and Dominicans, several from other Latin American backgrounds or mixed Puerto Rican and South Asian or Filipino descent. The majority of us had been born or raised in the United States in Spanish-speaking homes, but English was our primary, daily language. Arriving to the organization from different sectors of the community, we were wives, homemakers, and mothers with young children. Several of us had jobs in retail stores, offices, or hospitals, generally in clerical and administrative positions. Others were unemployed or were high school or college students. Several were lesbians. Some were survivors of domestic violence and drug addiction. We were also activists and community organizers.

The women in the Young Lords understood that to fight for social change, our organization had to mobilize the community and develop relationships with the people—with the politically, economically, and educationally disenfranchised. This meant living our political principles and working in coalition with other activists; it meant creating alliances with workers and students, and building new networks with artists and progressive policy makers. It also meant battling with city officials, self-serving politicians, and the New York City police.

The realities for Puerto Rican and other women of color at the time were extremely bleak with few prospects for a better future. Racist and sexist barriers dominated all facets of society. Educational opportunities were especially limited. The majority of workingwomen of color were steered into low-paying, unskilled, and semi-skilled jobs with few chances to advance. High numbers of Puerto Rican and African American single mothers with children survived on public assistance with no other options. Inevitably the early "survival programs" of the Young Lords responded to the needs of women. For example, the first Young Lords' clothing drive in East Harlem in 1969 reached out to 150 welfare mothers and distributed coats, sweaters, shoes, and other basic items to them. Successive free clothing programs aided similar families in need. The free breakfast programs fed the school-age children of single and working mothers. Door-to-door health testing in poor neighborhoods brought medical attention to children at risk for lead poisoning.

Convinced of the power of direct action, the women in the Young Lords became fighters, leaders, and political thinkers. We embraced three main principles in our organizing work: a belief in the right of poor people to economic, social, and political power; an emphasis on racial equality, self-determination, and human rights; and a feminist viewpoint that demanded a woman's right to control her reproduction and to share equally in all aspects of society. By imagining what society could be, we were energized to action.

Throughout New York City's poorest neighborhoods, young women in blue jeans proudly wearing the purple beret of the Young Lords were easily identifiable. We were out every day in Puerto Rican communities speaking with people who rarely received serious attention from anyone, listening to their opinions, and engaging them in discussions. Even in freezing cold weather, we sold *Palante*, the Young Lords' newspaper, on street corners, in subways, bodegas, shopping centers, clinics, and beauty salons, wherever people gathered. During the summer months, we sold the paper at city beaches and parks, during festivals and parades. In the mornings, we cooked breakfast for children; and, in the evenings, we taught political education classes in community centers, housing projects, and other neighborhood venues. We helped fellow members who could not read or write to develop these skills and stayed up late into the night with recruits who wanted to kick the heroin habit, helping them to become drug-free. Women also participated in takeovers, organized protests, and got arrested. In many ways, women were the backbone of the Young Lords.

BE SEEN, NOT HEARD

In the early days of the Young Lords Organization (YLO), the women members were practically invisible. . . . Women in the Young Lords were expected to be enthusiastic cheerleaders, clean offices, handle administrative tasks, and do the cooking, as well as perform as obedient sexual partners and wives. Women were expected to play supporting and submissive roles. . . .

Facing this reality, several of us in the East Harlem branch formed a Women's Caucus. . . . We studied the Young Lords' Thirteen-Point Program and Platform, especially Point 10, which stated: "We want equality for women. Machismo must be revolutionary . . . not oppressive." . . . "What is 'revolutionary machismo'?" a young woman asked hesitantly. After pausing to consider the question, a Puerto Rican woman answered. "I don't know." Shyly, one by one, we admitted that we didn't know. Finally, another woman said, "I'm not sure what it means either, because I've never known anything good to come out of machismo." She broke the ice, and we laughed. "How you gonna put 'revolutionary' and 'machismo' in the same sentence?" another woman added. "¡Eso fue un hombre! It had to be a man!" she joked. We laughed louder. "It's like saying revolutionary racism. It just doesn't make sense," an African American woman said. We agreed, this time more seriously.

We realized that although Point 10 made reference to machismo's ills in daily gender relations, including domestic violence and spousal abuse, it simply amended the "machismo" concept by placing the "revolutionary" qualifier in front of it. We recognized that "revolutionary machismo" was an oxymoron, that it actually reflected an embedded ambivalence about the equality of women. It preserved a gendered hierarchy that kept men in power without any commitment to the radical societal and personal transformation needed to make the liberation of women a reality and not just flowery rhetoric. "Would we accept the notion of "revolutionary racism"? The unanimous response was an unequivocal, "No!"

THE DEMANDS OF THE WOMEN'S CAUCUS

The Women's Caucus drafted a list of demands to present to the Central Committee; essentially, it was an appeal for respect, equal treatment, and accountability. A basic demand was to end the sexual objectification of women by men in the Young Lords. We considered ourselves comrades in struggle not sexual pawns or mindless bodies. Another concern was the absence of women in leadership. The caucus insisted that women be promoted to all levels, including the Central Committee. We sought to end the existing male-leader model, which perpetuated lack of confidence in women's abilities. . . .

The Women's Caucus also insisted that the political education program be expanded to include the study of feminist ideas and herstory, and the achievements of Puerto Rican, African American, and other women of color. Likewise, recognizing the important educational role of *Palante*, we advocated that the newspaper carry stories about women. Specifically, we pressed for half of all articles to be about issues affecting women of color and for 50 percent of the writers to be women. Lastly, we wanted the words "revolutionary machismo" removed from the Thirteen-Point Program and Platform. "*Machismo* is not revolutionary," we emphasized.

LESBIAN, GAY, BISEXUAL, AND TRANSGENDER YOUNG LORDS

The challenges of the Women's Caucus to conservative notions of gender identity and roles also opened the door for gay, lesbian, bisexual, and transgender (LGBT) women and men to join and participate in the Young Lords Party. Certainly, the acceptance of LGBT members in a paramilitary organization led by a male chauvinist hierarchy would not have been possible without the presence of a strong cadre of women defying and redefining the boundaries of traditional societal roles and demanding gender equality and justice.

The truth is that the idea of equality with gays was less acceptable to the community than women's equality. Although the Young Lords supported the participation of LGBT members in the organization, no self-identified LGBT member was ever appointed to the Central Committee or other leadership collectives. . . . Minister of information, Pablo "Yoruba" Guzmán acknowledged, "it's a lot quicker for people to accept the fact that sisters should be in the front of the struggle than saying that we're gonna have gay people in the organization." . . . The Young Lords wrote about the gay liberation struggle and contributed to the fight against backward ideas about sexual identity and orientation.

WOMEN AT THE FRONTLINES

In late 1970, the Central Committee published a revised version of the Thirteen-Point Program with a new section about women rights. It read: "We want Equality for Women. Down with Machismo and Male Chauvinism!" The words "revolutionary machismo" were removed.

As we battled to introduce feminist ideas to the Young Lords in 1970, we continued to organize in the community, run "serve the people" programs, and conduct political education classes. Women participated in setting up new branches. . . . Women played leading roles in health campaigns and joined in commandeering a mobile TB truck, rerouting it to East Harlem where hundreds of residents were tested. When Lincoln Hospital announced staff and service cutbacks, women joined in the takeover of the facility demanding worker-community control and quality health services. Women helped to mobilize 10,000 people to the United Nations bringing international attention to the colonial status of Puerto Rico and coordinated a national conference where 1,000 college and high school students planned "Liberate Puerto Rico Now" committees and networks. After Young Lord Julio Roldán was found hung in a jail cell, women in the Young Lords took up guns alongside men in the Second People's Church ready to be locked up or die. From storefronts to schools, hospitals, churches and streets, women in the Young Lords were at the frontlines.

THE WOMEN'S UNION

In 1971, a Women's Union was formed. . . . As a unifying document, the women developed a twelve-point program. Focused on the needs and interests of low-income women of color, the program called for full employment, equal pay, employer-provided childcare, and compensation for housework—all demands still not met today. It also advocated for the rights of sex workers and drug-addicted sisters, the most vulnerable and oppressed women of color in society—the women society treated as the most disposable.

The commitment to personal transformation led us to look inward as well. We, too, consumed, and unconsciously accepted, the dominant stereotypes about societal and family roles reserved for women of color. Collectively, we scrutinized the prejudices embedded in the national psyche about our abilities, physical appearance, and skin color, drummed into our minds, hearts, and bodies since birth, passed down from generation to generation by families, media, and all other institutions. As women of color, we grappled with the attitudes of inferiority and feelings of inadequacy these caused. Our passivity often showed as timidity or fear of questioning authority. Facing deep-rooted self-negativity also meant challenging complicity with practices that placed a higher value on men. "Male-identified females" favored men and gave more credence to their views; they automatically accepted men as more adept leaders and thinkers, believing that women were less capable. As we deconstructed the negative narratives about women, we became more determined to fight for social change.

The members of the Women's Union understood that talk meant nothing without action. Both women and men had to act to achieve gender equality and justice. Not all women were sisters simply because we were of the same gender, and men could be allies. In our struggles to achieve justice and equality for women, we never lost sight of the fact that men of color were our fathers, brothers, sons, friends, husbands, and lovers who were also oppressed by the same capitalist system and institutions as we were.

SUMMARY

Women joined the Young Lords Organization to make revolution, to fight poverty, racism, and the exploitation of women, and to free Puerto Rico from U.S. colonialism. With visionary ideas, a warrior spirit, and loving hearts, women performed leading and significant roles. Our battle was against capitalism and imperialism, and the powerful forces in control of the world's resources. We pursued the "revolution within the revolution" uniting the struggles for women's liberation with demands for social, economic, and racial justice.

Women in the Young Lords led campaigns to achieve better living conditions and opportunities for the most vulnerable and exploited women in our communities—working poor, working class students, mothers on welfare, women in prison, drug addicted women, and prostitutes. Differences among women of color were acknowledged, and we believed that improving the circumstances of the poorest and most oppressed among us would transform society and benefit everyone.

(Edited excerpt from *Through the Eyes of Rebel Women:*
The Young Lords, 1969-1976.
Red Sugarcane Press, Inc., 2016)

The Women's Union
Twelve-Point Program

THE YOUNG LORDS PARTY

1) We believe in the liberation of all Puerto Ricans—liberation on the island and inside the U.S.

2) We believe in the self-determination of all third world people.

3) We want equality for women—down with machismo and sexism.

4) We want full employment and equal pay for all women with day care facilities provided by the work institution.

5) We want an end to the present welfare system; community-worker boards must be established in all welfare centers to ensure the protection of women and their needs.

6) We want an end to the particular oppression of prostitutes and drug-addict sisters.

7) We want the withdrawal of the American military force from our communities and an end to their sexual abuse of women.

8) We want freedom for all political prisoners and prisoners of war and an end to the sexual brutalization and torture enforced on sisters by prison officials.

9) We want an end to the experimentation and genocide committed on sisters through sterilization, forced abortions, contraceptives, and unnecessary gynecological exams.

10) We want a true education of our story as women.

11) We believe in the right to defend ourselves against rapes, beatings, muggings, and general abuse.

12) We want a socialist society.

PART 6.

SAVE THE EARTH.
FIGHT FOR OUR HOMES!

This Is My Home

VICKIE VÉRTIZ

I don't want to start off broken   But my pencil is running out
That's OK   We have more lead in the yard

My home is   I can't breathe   Surrounded by sound walls
you   can't   hear
          In that quiet, a child finishes their homework,   closing a good
          thing

The LA River ends in Vernon   After Slauson, the friends of the river
run out, too

          The death stench in our water   In our jobs   In the classroom
          Everywhere a gas leak

          This is my home

My mother and brother are ten thousand truck miles   Why won't
their coughs go away?   The freeway, my lover says
          Coffins with windows

          Pig fat rendered into lipsticks
          We're bottling the leftovers   Crates of rotten chitlins will
                detonate over San Marino lawns

When I took Amá to the garden in that city   she looked out the
windshield at their grass and said   *They don't have earthquakes
here, do they, Chata?*
          They do, I said   They just don't have to feel them

This is our home: arsenic fairy dust on wedding cookies
        A student plucks a lead bloom and sharpens in the lungs
        Cancer berries cluster and   It's no use, this poem
I lost my parents to the pollution   And no one's come
        to clean my yard

You can have our methane clouds   Windshield tacos
The river is a stream and   the freeway's always running
We are death flower orchards, twenty-one square miles   opening and
closing   Our miscarriages bubble and thin into glue

I've never felt worthless

We plant broken glass in the riverbed   we dream about dabbing lead
perfume behind your clean pink ears   Jumping our skateboards
off the cement and into your   bright
white
        teeth

My home is invisible wild lupine   though blooms purple with tumor
pistils   This is our bougainvillea triplex   This is our date palm
This is our jacaranda   This is my home

We stole the whole thing up   That sushi you're eating?
It's cueritos from the Farmer John's
Who are the fools?   Not this nopal light

The student is boiling our water   to get rid of your poison
        The start? The finish?   The PE mile you had to run?
        It's here   A river's reverie
The you and me—
        Then   water

(First published in UCLA's Bozalta Magazine, 2016)

Poison Beneath Our Feet

A I D A   S A L A Z A R

Since 1922, Exide Technologies, a battery melting plant in Vernon, CA,
deposited toxic waste in the soil, air and water in Southeast Los Angeles.
Five areas surrounding its 15-acre plant were contaminated, including
Maywood, Boyle Heights, Bell, Commerce, Huntington Park.[1]

My father sits quietly eating a salad I've prepared for him. He
reads his Bible. He chews and swallows – kale, green apple, endives,
sunflower seeds in a citrus dressing – all as foreign to his body as his
metastasized cancer.   I live four hundred miles away in Northern
California and I've come home, like I once did for my mother, to now
guide him through alternative cancer treatments based in raw food and
herbs. I've come back to the family compound in Maywood, a tiny
incorporated "city" in inner Southeast Los Angeles. Three small
structures make up our childhood home—a small three-bedroom
house, a two-car garage with a studio apartment upstairs and a one-
bedroom bungalow way out back. Since their separation, the Catholic
equivalent of a divorce, *Papi* and *Mami* each occupy different
dwellings on the same lot. Mami lives in the main house where she
spent a lifetime as homemaker hustling side jobs to help feed the seven
children she bore. Papi, lives in the studio apartment in a skyward
hermitage somewhat estranged since his infidelities created an
enormous fissure in our family. They are as the Mexican refrain says,
juntos pero no revueltos. Beneath these structures, they share the same
land, a soil that has collected our familial memories for four decades,
as well as Mexican immigrants and toxic waste to the brim. Mami and
Papi both have cancer.
   Mami once took one bite of an avocado that had been smuggled
to the United States from her hometown in Mexico and its flavor was
so delicious she knew right then that she would use the pit and sprout a

---

1. Barboza, Tony. "How a Battery Recycler Contaminated L.A.-area
Homes for Decades." Los Angeles Times, December 21, 2015. Retrieved from
www.LosAngelesTimes.com, September 1, 2016.

tree of her own. We had lived in the Maywood house only seven years when she planted the pit. Now the tree is like an enormous canopy that shades the entire back yard, and the neighbor's yard and incessantly sheds its huge dried leaves. My father's apartment is a perched tree house because nearly every window opens up to the branches of our avocado tree that is three stories tall. Morning doves often mate there but in Maywood, there are no squirrels. There are no raccoons or possums like there are in Oakland, something that in our childhood we did not know should have been there. For years, we ate the *aguacate's* green flesh in all manner of recipes – guacamole, in salsas, on the side with rice and beans, or simply in a taco with salt, lemon, and chile. We trusted in the tree's big beautiful fruit.

Papi's cancer is in his prostate. The cancer has seeped to surrounding areas. They want to remove his glands to which he agrees without question, then chemo, and radiation. He believes doctor knows best. Never mind that he witnessed how seventeen years ago, Mami defied the doctors who told her she would be dead in three months, by following alternative natural therapies. My sister insisted that we try with Papi what we did with Mami before the surgery. Papi surprisingly agreed. And so, since I helped lead the path for Mami, I am with him now, juicing, preparing avocado salad, and mixing herbs.

I used to think that Mami's cancer was from residual poisoning. When my parents first bought this house in the 70s, very soon after the race restrictions were lifted in Maywood and White Flight was in full effect, among the many things we inherited with the house was a healthy population of roaches. Our parents decided to tent the entire property and fumigate with pesticides that I'm certain are illegal now. When we returned to our house, every fiber, dish, and surface—be it wood, plastic, linoleum, or glass—reeked of a nauseatingly strong chemical odor. Mami took to washing and scrubbing all that she could. We slept with the windows opened and had to throw out ruined items. Yet the smell persisted in our books, shoes, in the attic and basement, penetrated in the grain of the wood, the walls and in the crevices Mami's cleaning did not reach. She was home more than any of us. We would scatter to school or work or play outside for six or more hours each day while she stayed home with the remnant fumes of the insecticides. She is still there now. It was during college that I learned of the dangers of insecticides on people through the plight of the United Farm Workers. Naturally, it stood to reason, that she would be the one in our family to develop cancer—Angiosarcoma—a cancer so rare that it afflicts one in a million people. I held that theory along with improper eating as the principal culprits for years. Now that cancer has come to Papi, that theory is questionable. Papi, after all, spent the least amount of time at home as he often worked two shifts at the Rehrig Pacific—the plastic crate-making factory in Vernon, where many of our relatives from Zacatecas also worked. My uncle, Martin, lost three of his fingers and one man that we know of, his life, to their assembly line machines. Still, these factories were the first step for many Mexican immigrants in the journey to attain the proverbial American dream. I question hard work, lack of real health care, poor food choices and I can't arrive at one source. I can only think of providing this food medicine now. I know this will heal them but I know better. I know there is more.

It is never uncommon to wake to a deathly stench in the air in Maywood. It is a combination of dead pigs from Farmer John's slaughtering house/meat processing plant, with the fertilizer factory just off of the 710 freeway or the hundreds of factories who look like a series of chain smokers across Vernon's horizon. When I was a child, whenever we got onto the freeway, heading north, we could clearly see the San Gabriel mountain range so closely it seemed we could be there in a few short minutes. Over the years, however, the smog grew so thick it became difficult to see where the mountains were, where north lies. Papi was a smoker though Mami never allowed him to smoke indoors because she was sensitive to the smell. He smoked on the porch in the evenings. He finally gave up smoking twenty years ago. One night, during an unusually cold evening, he was freezing outside and puffing away. He saw the absurdity in his suffering and he quit right then and there. The air that surrounds my father now is not much different since he quit, despite the oxygen the avocado tree gives.

I am downstairs, in Mami's house checking my email in between preparing Papi's juices and meals and she gets a visitor. It is the Los Angeles County health department worker who is canvassing the neighborhood, seeking permission from each of the residents to test the property for lead and arsenic contamination. I read the document, which is both in Spanish and in English that briefly explains that Exide Technologies will be paying for the complete replacement of any soil or item found to be contaminated with lead or arsenic inside or outside of the home. Mami is devastated, not because there might be lead in the soil, but because it means that they would have to uproot every single one of the dozens of plants that she has so painstakingly grown into a bountiful *jardin* over the years, including the avocado tree. She mournfully whispers, "*mis plantas,*" as her eyes fill with tears.

After reading over the document, I am outraged too. How long has this been happening? Why had no one stopped the toxic spills? The county worker shakes his head and says, "It's done. Our only recourse is to clean it up." I encourage Mami to sign. But she argues, "What if my neighbors do not sign, then what good does it do to get rid of my plants if there is still lead in their soil?" This is an excellent point. The county worker says it is to their benefit and it will not cost them a dime. "They'll sign Señora. They'll sign, if they know you've signed." She shakes her head no. "If you don't agree to it now, there is no telling when they will run out of money for clean up." I suspect the county worker knows more than he can tell us.

Papi has no idea about this transaction. In his birdhouse, he is detoxing in a bad way like a heroine addict. He is running to the bathroom, the leg cramps keep him up at night; he is fatigued and shaky when he walks. These are all healing crises that he will undergo as he detoxifies, not easy for anyone by any means but ultimately regenerating and not damaging like chemo. It is the reason why I must be here with him. Mami uncrosses her arms, which she held as if hugging herself, and signs the document. The county worker leaves us to wonder, how long have we eaten from this garden. We count all of the fruit trees and vegetables in our yard—guamara, apricot, guayabas, avocado, tomatoes, chiles, guache—that grew in what we believed was perfectly good soil. We never gave the level of poison that might lie within a thought until now.

I go out on the porch and look down the bungalow-filled street, the street where as a child, I ran barefoot in a pack with my siblings, unaware of the deadly contamination beneath our feet. My eyes land on Judy's house. Judy was my childhood best friend who lived eight houses down who developed cancer in a toe when we were in Middle School. Though they removed the toe and put the poor child through chemotherapy, the cancer persisted. When a new tumor grew in the arch of her foot, they amputated her entire foot. Judy told me she did not know what the word amputate meant until after the surgery when she awoke to find that her foot was gone. She was only eleven. Then the faces of so many of our neighbors who also have suffered from serious diseases appear in my mind—my sister in law's parents; Luis, a high school friend; friends who worked in the factories nearby; Doña Marie; Lolo the kid next door; the countless ailing people that have come to Mami to ask her what she did to survive her illness. I think of their challenged lives with rare cancers, mental disorders, birth defects, blood disorders, autism and the realization chokes me. I wonder how many families have been poisoned, how many continue to eat from their own contaminated fruit trees.

When I return to Papi's apartment, he is waking from a nap. I don't tell him about the worker's visit. Instead I begin to prepare his next batch of organic juice. I smile. I don't want to discourage him now. I look at the perfect carrots and green apples that have been imported from some organic farm far away from Maywood. I want to believe that Papi will heal this cancer, like my mother does daily by buying organic foods they can hardly afford on their social security incomes. I struggle with continuing this natural treatment. Is it futile? Mami's cancer though we began to fight it naturally, seventeen years ago, remains a nagging though no longer life-threatening presence. Could these natural treatments work if the very soil beneath their feet, the very air they breathe is contaminated? I fight anger, sadness as they churn inside my head and as I breathe in and out the soot-filled air in Maywood. It is the air and land of my childhood and that my parents have endured for nearly forty years.

I wish for an abundance of Santa Ana winds, for storms, to move my parents to Oakland. What really could cleanse this Southeast LA earth? Suddenly, the wisdom of connection shakes me and the distance between my parents and I shrinks—we share the same air, the same soil. There is no difference between what is done to the earth in Southeast LA or Oakland—we will all eventually feel its affects. The earth will metastasize if poisoned long enough. I curse batteries, all of the cars, the same car that brought me close to help heal my parents. I curse Exide Technologies, the agencies that allowed them to continue to operate and greedy corporate profits. The level of injustice to us all is sickening and my level of impotence to help even more. In my angry distraction, I cut my hand on the juicer's blade. I grab a pinch of cayenne and put it right on the cut. It stops bleeding immediately. I am then reminded in the body's ability to heal—knowledge that I know well. I am reminded that there is medicine to be given, to Papi, to Mami and to the earth.

I continue to wash and cut carrots. I run them through the juicer, pour a tall glass for Papi. As I approach him with the organic orange-colored drink in my hand, he smiles at me. Without asking, he opens his mouth and I pour in two droppersful of detox tincture. He winces, takes a deep breath, and begins to sip the carrot juice; his graying eyebrows lift above his large eyes. He breathes. He says, "Gracias *hija*, gracias."

(2017)

How to Build a Funeral Pyre

Leticia Hernández-Linares

The pyre in my chest is old. The custom of burning
someone beloved, into a small pile of ash, a new, step

by step process. My limbs affixed to the undertow
of la calle, yet a singeing awaits of this internally lodged place.

To secure a decent burn, the detail of construction
will determine the purity of smoke and breath.

The need for the stacking of wood, not intended
for the removal of family and bone, from decades of dwelling.

Entire blocks leveled, not like a bombing, in so many world corners,
of other tongued children, during before times in West Philly, of black

bodies. In this version, brashness ignites in the open, any immigrant
occupant will do. Brazen, the flames illuminate insurance awards

that make for a successful smolder. A mother's resolve
to cross whatever amount of miles for any spin of better, the indignity,

the disorientation, the turning of a bag of beans into gold, vanished
by their millions sweeping us under the howl of a Bart train,

the kind routing things treasured to the end of the line with a speed
that turns flesh and familiar neighborhood melodies into a pile of ash.

"31,007 housing units in San Francisco have faced 2,654 fires since 2005. The Bayview had the most units affected, with 3,437, followed by the Mission, with 2,788. (The two blocks of Mission Street between 18th and 20th streets have garnered 59 violations in the past decade, the worst record in the city, *the Examiner* recently found.) Downtown/Civic Center comes in third, with 2,544, followed closely by Western Addition, which had 2,288 units affected by fires."

(Anti-Eviction Mapping Project, 2016.
http://www.antievictionmappingproject.net/fires.html)

Ms. 99% - A Reluctant Super Hero Learns from Real Super Mujeres

LENINA NADAL

Every Latinx chica should have the opportunity to play a superhero. I will never forget the time I was given the chance to make a meme into flesh and play a character named, "Ms. 99." The meme was "Bank vs. America."

The year was 2012. As the newly-hired Communications Director of the Right to the City Alliance and a member of a national team of social justice communicators, our task was to call out the villains of the housing foreclosure crisis and deliver a narrative about the forced displacement caused by banks when they played with people's homes like game pieces on a monopoly board. We received constant calls from people who needed help, and many of our local organizations could not meet the need. A year after Occupy Wall Street, we needed to keep the flame strong for all the families who lost their homes and win as much as we could from the banks who profited and zapped the wealth of mainly Black and Latinx communities, though the entire country was affected. We looked for a creative way to tell this story that could influence public policy and aid hundreds of struggling families.

Our national and local campaign strategies included online petitions, occupying homes, and moving people back into their homes when police or other officials came to evict them. At community meetings, hundreds of families shared stories of how they were affected and received legal support to fight their cases in court.

We researched and found that the largest bank in the United States, the Bank of America, had engaged in predatory lending and illegal foreclosures. We learned of the Bank of America shareholders' meeting in Charlotte, North Carolina, and a decision was made to disrupt it with hecklers to shame the bank for forcibly foreclosing on families to make a quick buck. The shareholders' meeting would be a culminating event, an opportunity for families, who often dealt with the embarrassment of foreclosure in isolation, to join with people facing similar situations all over the country. It was also a chance to boost the movement with imaginative storytelling and communications.

For more than two months, we planned. After an intense process with several community organizations in partnership with the Center for Story Based Strategy, we decided on the meme of "Bank vs. America." The "fight" would take place near the shareholders' meeting in Charlotte. I wrote a script to be performed for street theatre with the objective of creating a spectacle that would shut down a major street intersection. Ms. 99%, the protagonist, would represent America. In typical hero's journey format, she was a reluctant heroine who would fall, be beaten, and then get up again to fight and win. She would battle her toughest adversary, Brian "Big Banks" Moynihan, the CEO of Bank of America. We crafted our demands to the bank, which included the reduction of loan principal, increased funding for affordable housing, and the disinvestment of the bank from the fossil fuel industry. The skit would underline these points and show the bank's victims rejoicing in the streets. The mainstream media was already buzzing with the "Bank vs. America" meme. The NY Times called it brilliant public relations.

As a single mom paying more than 30% of my income to rent, I too was one of the millions in the United States paying too much for housing. As I spoke to people across the country, I saw that Latinas were front and center in the housing foreclosure crisis. As primary breadwinners or single mothers with children, Latinas seeking financial stability for themselves and their families were vulnerable to manipulation by predatory lenders. In one case, a Puerto Rican-Dominican widow had purchased a two-story home in the Bronx, an investment that meant everything to her. She was wheelchair-bound and had difficulty getting around. She had lost her husband to cancer, lived with her 22-year-old son, and had raised her five children in the house. She was a proud homeowner. The house represented her wealth and meant she did not have to live at the whim of a landlord. She dutifully made the mortgage payments, and then one day, she received a letter from Bank of America saying that the loan company she had borrowed from had been taken over. Her home would be foreclosed if she did not make the new payments, which were increased by 100%. She was scared; but she resolved to fight the bank. She told me of other women homeowners in the Bronx who read the foreclosure letters, panicked, and moved out of their homes. But in her case, she engaged in an intense struggle, and the Bank of America met with her and negotiated a new agreement. It took courage and protests, a press strategy, and an awareness of her rights to force the bank to the table. She was definitely on my mind as we prepared to raise hell at the national Bank of America shareholders' meeting.

Based on the initial script, we created posters and a trailer promo advertising the fight between Ms. 99% and Big Banks. Volunteers acted the roles and did costume design and props. Our internal security team created the boxing ring in the streets.

Ms. 99% was my favorite acting role ever. I was both in a DIY boxing ring on a "stage" and taking over a city at the same time. Once a super hero, you carry with you the mission to serve the community with a commitment that is visible and supportive.

And so what was the result? What did the action lead to? Most importantly, it launched a national Right to the City campaign to fight the gentrification and housing crisis that continues. *The New York Times, Huffington Post, Reuters*, and the *Associated Press* reported the event and the issues. In the national press, it was in the top two news stories of the day. The photo of our boxing ring fight inspired spectacle action theorists everywhere.

I often hold to a rubric called the 3 Rs to guide my work. It stands for Real, Radical and Relevant. *Real politics* is organizing based on actual lived experience. It means working with the people who are the most affected by the issues and learning from them to ground the political objective. It looks to raise awareness but also to transform the material conditions or create options.

Radical politics means shifting cultural values and consciousness and moving in the direction of a clear alternative to capitalism, for example, a socialist and/or democratically shared economy where wealth is available to all in a tangible way.

The last factor relates to narrative campaign strategy and communications, is it *relevant*? Does the political work resonate at the time? Does it feel urgent to what is moving people? In the case of the housing and affordability crisis, Occupy Wall Street was instrumental in pointing out the vast inequity in U.S. society by popularizing the slogan, "We are the 99%." It lifted the curtain to display the greed of the 1% of the global population that was amassing the world's wealth for themselves.

We must continue to lift up big ideas at the same time that we deal with the real conditions and struggles facing people. In our communications and outreach, we have possibilities in the realm of artistic expression, comic books, and tweets to deliver communiqués. We must let our imagination run wild with stories that build awareness and show a path to action without forgetting to love each other profoundly.

(2017)

Showdown in Charlotte: Bank vs. America
at Bank of America Shareholders Meeting
View at www.youtube.com /watch?v=AuYkrT0u2hU.)

PART 7.

GRASSROOTS ORGANIZING
& REBEL IMAGINATION

"Gloria's Tree" represents a cypress tree in Santa Cruz, California that Gloria Anzaldúa visited daily. Its roots stretch out into the air as if they are reaching towards the ocean. The foliage is made up of her poetry and prose, the fruition of her growth as a writer.

Claudia Sofia Garriga López

Gloria's Tree

CLAUDIA SOFIA GARRIGA LÓPEZ

"Gloria's Tree"   claudia sofía 2017

Credo

Florencia Milito

I believe in herds of wild, red horses,
imagination as counterpoint to suffering,
purveyor of empathy.
In ritual when it cracks open
into yellow sky, rising
from the illusory fog
of the quotidian,
in Neruda's book of questions.

I believe forgetting our mortality
is hardwired,
leads to other kinds of forgetting,
history repeating itself,
renders us myopic,
never again a hollow promise
or talisman.

I believe in the rare gifts
of the unconscious,
burnt oranges,
dips into the sea of the collective,
in the basic decency of so many ordinary folk
and the ruthlessness of power.

I believe in lost causes and whistleblowers,
the lyric, the cobalt-blue lotus in my dream,
elusive, this persistent compass.

(2017)

Maduros y Verdes:
Venues for All Voices

MAGDALENA GÓMEZ

When I arrived in western Massachusetts from my native New York City in autumn of 1989, I was mesmerized by the natural beauty of the landscapes and stunned by the noises and nuances of bigotry. "You're a Puerto Rican? Really? You don't look it." Those words were usually stated as if they were a compliment. The looks of welcome to my melanin deprived body quickly disappeared at my unapologetic pronunciation of my entire name in the full glory of a Bronx Boricua Spanish dialect. Cringe: "Oh, uh, where are you from?" Smolder: "I can't pronounce that. Do you have a nickname?" Condescension: "Ohhhh, that's such a . . . pretty name." Assimilationist abbreviations ended in my youth. "No, I don't." Those three little words quickly separated the wheat from the chaff. The chaff always offered options as if I simply hadn't thought of any ways I could circumcise my name on their behalf. "How about Maggie?" "Maddie?" "I'll call you Magda." Silence. "No, you won't."

When I shared some of these and other related stories with my friend Beth, she said, "You used to live in New York. Now you live in America." Nailed it. This is not to say that you won't find issues of bigotry and class in NYC, but I didn't constantly have to navigate through insult and assault on a daily basis both personally and as a pro-active witness. Living in Western Massachusetts has been a lot more work than I ever imagined.

Living in the house that my white male partner had rented, I didn't know it would be like to seek an apartment. I expected Northampton, known as woman friendly and called "Paradise City" to be a cinch. The highlights: prospective landlord calls one of my previous ones: "Is she the kind that will destroy the apartment?" Another prospect: "My best friend is Mexican and passes for white when he's apartment hunting. He thinks it's hilarious." I left exhausted after giving a brief lesson on internalized colonialism and a slop bucket full of reasons why there's nothing funny about it. By the time I rented a place, the excitement of moving had gathered dust. I moved again and was told to shut the windows, too much laughter coming from the house. Once when students of color came to visit the downstairs neighbor railed: "You ruined my day. The sounds coming from your place were so horrible I had to spend the day in my car." Soon after that an eviction notice was slipped under the door; fought and overturned. That was the 1990's.

I now live on the south side of the "tofu curtain" (thank you, Brian Hale) in Springfield, the fourth largest, and one of the most economically oppressed cities in the state. I live here with my partner of twenty-five years, and I have met some of the most extraordinary people I know in this enigmatic city, replete with artists, creatives, innovators, and thinkers. A city where the population is over 65% people of color, but the same well-heeled poverty pimp dinosaurs still roam and rule. They have yet to receive their extinction memo, but it's on the way, thanks to a more enlightened younger generation and marginalized activists who've been resisting for a very long time.

When we first arrived in 1999 and purchased a home here, Springfield was one of the most segregated cities in the country. I have always loved a challenge as long as I can hear multiple languages while taking it on. We found a house on what may have been the most integrated block in the city at that time: Puerto Ricans, Jews, Irish, Italians, African Americans, Dominicans, and Vietnamese families with all the beautiful sounds of children playing on the commons blessing our days. One year, I dressed up on Halloween and gave out 150 ribbon wrapped bags of candy; this past year, the doorbell didn't ring once. Fear of violence and addiction to screens keep the kids indoors, as their bodies fester the inevitable diseases of the sedentary. Adults grow weary of too much work for too little money and a *feral* government, scavenging from the *tripas* of the poor to feed the rich.

The segregation narrative in Springfield is changing, but the mindset of ethnocentric clannishness still persists. Racism is still palpable, a fact exacerbated by class divisions even within the same ethnic groups. Lessons from the Master and Patrón must be schooled out of our bones and our educational system has never been suited to the task. The tyranny that prevails in Springfield provides a microcosmic view of our nation; we have been coerced and seduced into living isolated, myopic, self-protective lives.

My husband Jim and I decided to begin an arts salon in our home where artists could socialize and network, have readings, art showings, break bread and feel more connected to the community and their peers. Friends came from our immediate area, the region, and reaching into NYC. Preparing for gatherings of anywhere from 20 to 75 people was a great deal of work, and we did it gladly. World-class musicians jammed in the living room and backyard releasing glorious sounds from djembes, congas, cuatros, guitars, flutes, trombones, saxophones, maracas, and once the Holyoke Steel Band set up and played in the driveway. There was dancing, laughter, an abundance of food, everyone brought something in addition to what we provided, and neighbors only complained when the music stopped. There was not another a single place in the city where diverse and intergenerational artists could interact and where LGBTQ artists could be fully out and safe.

Jim and I saw so many positive results from the salons that I decided, at the age of 53, to start a theater ensemble for youth who would have opportunities to collaborate with some of the great artists we know. I did some research to learn that the city had never had their own Latin@ theater, despite the fact that the city's Latin@ population was at the time, close to 39% and growing. I had actually attempted to secure a performance space from the time I arrived in 1999, but being new to the city, I really didn't know who to approach or how to do it. Most of my livelihood was on the college circuit as a performance poet and keynote speaker, so I wasn't home long enough to make the full court press. I kept the dream awake and in 2006 approached a businessman who spoke at a local community college, H. Edgar Alejandro. He spoke about the Latino Breakfast Club (LBC) and their Latino Scholarship program. I pitched my idea, sent it in writing, and he accepted. My vision was an arts-based program run by youth for youth. We began rent free in the basement of the Springfield YMCA in the autumn of 2007.

In 2008 the LBC sponsored our official inauguration at the Springfield Museums, where we also launched youth scripted productions on issues they identified, in the 287-seat theater, which had previously been underutilized. Museum attendance increased exponentially after our productions, according to Kay Simpson, now the Executive Director of the Museums. Within a couple of years we were in a 10,000 square foot studio space, provided rent free by realtor, NAI Plotkin Associates. We are now the theater in residence at the Bing Arts Center. Space, volunteers, guest artists, refreshments for events, media coverage, money to pay for basic expenses: what we need to keep going keeps showing up. AmherstMedia.org, where my husband is the Executive Director, has documented our first ten years so far. We are currently partnered with the Office of Multicultural Affairs at Springfield College that has committed ongoing support providing refreshments for our monthly open mic series, which features youth from the entire region, reaching into Connecticut. The majority of our youth members have graduated from college, several have gotten advanced degrees; some have their own businesses, and every one of them are productive leaders within their chosen fields. Those who have returned, and those who have just arrived, are moving Teatro V!da forward, and I know they have the skills to do it without me.

Wherever it all lands, I know that we have been part of the on-going changing narrative in our region and have inspired new artistic community growth. Our first Poet in Residence, María Luisa Arroyo, became the first Poet Laureate of Springfield–we've had many historic firsts resulting from our collective work, including Springfield's first LGBTQ open mic at the Bing Arts Center.

Our members have had leadership and artistic roles in community; academia; radio; television; stage; print; libraries; conferences; street fairs; health related events; have been honored by City Hall Proclamations; won scholarships; and have been published and commissioned by contract as writers, performers and presenters; they were integral to the public dialogue and re-imagining the city after the devastating 2011 tornado. Teatro V!da youth, took leadership roles in citywide meetings with over 300 adults. Sixteen year-old Gabriel Cifuentes politely told the room, in part: "We've done good work here today and great ideas have come from it. We the youth will be watching you. We are holding you accountable for putting these ideas into action." Providing venue for the voices and ideas of young people in always a good idea and a sound investment.

(2017)

Power and Pride: A Poet's Notes On Marching at the Puerto Rican Day Parade

MARIA TERESA "MARIPOSA" FERNÁNDEZ

Marching in the Puerto Rican Day Parade was epiphany-like and beautiful, almost a religious experience, and a deeply political act for me. Yes, I am a poet. Marching in the parade propelled my political development. It provided a space where I deepened my commitment to work towards the freedom of Puerto Rico and Puerto Ricans. The experience connected me to the collective consciousness of my people in a way that being a writer cannot. The electric feeling of Boricua pride in its fullest and most creative expression can be described as a fruit that is the absolute ripest on this day, colorful and sweet. Match that feeling with the rebellious pride that commands respect, calls for freedom, and honors our ancestors who did the same. The combination of celebrating our culture with political organizing is an important strategy: a way to raise consciousness and build power.

I do not come from a political family. I am a second generation Puerto Rican, born and raised in the Bronx, and I did not have a clue about Puerto Rican history until I was in my early 20s. My inklings about being Puerto Rican were limited to family experiences, and my Tío handing me a copy of Piri Thomas' *Down These Mean Streets* when I was 14.

I cannot remember how many times I have marched in the Puerto Rican Day Parade, but some parades I will never forget. The first time I marched was in June 1997. I was in my mid-20s and a member of the ProLibertad Campaign to free the Puerto Rican political prisoners and prisoners of war. At the time, there were 16 prisoners, eleven men and five women, in federal penitentiaries throughout the United States. They were not convicted of any violent crime. They were charged with seditious conspiracy—a thought crime—of wanting Puerto Rico to be free. I had read their stories in, *Prisoners of Colonialism* by Ronald Fernández, a book that brought me to tears and blew my mind. The vicious history of political repression in Puerto Rico and criminalization of the independence movement enraged me. By this point, I had become aware of my own mis-education and had gained political consciousness. This singular experience, of marching in the parade for the first time, solidified my sense of belonging, and my knowledge of self; hence, I owned my identity.

I remember when we built the ProLibertad float. Together, an old friend and I constructed a huge replica of the Statue of Liberty's head, her eyes covered with the Puerto Rican flag. Her crown was adorned with machetes bearing the names of each political prisoner. Some people loved it. Others were shocked, but it got people's attention, which is what we aimed to do.

It was a political act to march then, and it is now. To wave the Puerto Rican flag, and proudly shout "Boricua!" at the top of your lungs with a mission. It also meant facing the internalized oppression of our people and our families. I faced a lot of the same ignorance we still deal with today. Back in the mid-1990s, when I collected signatures to free the Puerto Rican political prisoners, a few angry *viejos y viejas* yelled at me, as they spit on the ground and cursed us.

"Esa gente van a pudrirse en la cárcel. Son terroristas." I remember clutching my clipboard, feeling a mixture of anger, sadness, and horror.

I also had to deal with my mother's disapproval. I faced her head on in the kitchen as she angrily waved letters in my face; letters with federal penitentiary return addresses.

"María, what are you doing? What is the meaning of this? Writing to prisoners?! *¿Tu 'ta loca?"* I'm sure her anger came from fear that I would wind up in prison. The fact of political prisoners promotes fear; this is how fascist governments discourage dissent. Naturally, there were times when I felt fear, but I never let it stop me. I grew a stronger backbone instead.

In the 1990s, the Puerto Rican Day Parade committee put the marchers for political causes and community organizations at the back of the parade. We had to show up at 8:00 a.m. and waited for hours for our turn. It always bothered me that the New York Police Department (NYPD) Hispanic Society and politicians were at the front while community organizers, activists, and cultural workers were last. Big companies like Goya also got prominent prime time placements in the lineup.

In 2000, the Puerto Rican Day Parade was dedicated to the struggle of Vieques and to Don Pedro Albizu Campos. Doña Lolita

Lebron marched with us, and I remember seeing her giving out *flores y ramas*, surrounded by a sea of Viequense flags, marching with the Viequense people to demand that the United States Navy cease bombing practices on the island. A huge statue of Don Pedro, sculpted by the renowned Puerto Rican artist, Antonio Mantorell, led the contingent. But that year the media totally ignored the parade's powerful political message. Instead, they vilified and blamed the parade for an incident that occurred after it was over when groups of men, some of them Latino, groped and sexually assaulted women in Central Park.

For a period of time after 2000, political groups decided not to march. Why? The New York Police Department began to demand names, addresses, and phone numbers of all marchers.

I marched in the parade again in 2014 with *33 Mujeres*, a movement of Puerto Rican women to free then political prisoner, Oscar López Rivera. His case had gained international attention when Archbishop Desmond Tutu and Pope Francis joined the call for his release.

Three years later in 2017, the board of the National Puerto Rican Day Parade announced that Oscar López Rivera would be honored as a freedom fighter and Puerto Rican hero. The media quickly rushed to discredit and bully the parade board and engaged in a campaign of outright lies, ignoring the fact that Oscar was *never charged*, and *never convicted* of any act of violence. The corporate media sought to not only criminalize this courageous Puerto Rican but also the independence movement itself. Big corporations like Goya and others, civil service agencies, some politicians, and the NYPD Hispanic Society declared they would boycott the parade.

How fitting that the New York Police Department unwittingly ousted itself from the parade. Ironically, the NYPD's so-called boycott was the fruition of a seed planted long ago—the idea that the Puerto Rican Day Parade should not be helmed by the police but by the true defenders of the Puerto Rican people.[1]

---

1. In 1971 the Young Lords Party (YLP) attempted to interrupt the long history of the New York Police Department marching at the front of the parade. "Poor people, instead of the police, should lead the parade to protest the city's budget cuts and layoffs, and US colonialism in Puerto Rico," the Young Lords said. A seed was planted. The attempt backfired when a violent confrontation with the police ensued; twenty persons were arrested and many

The venomous reaction to the Puerto Rican Day Parade Board and their naming Oscar López Rivera as *Prócer de la Libertad*, National Freedom Hero, a title he later graciously bestowed on the people, showed how the government and its apparatuses wanted to keep us subservient, small and unheard. How dare we be proud. How dare we celebrate our hero. We must see the corporate and media's reaction within the historical context of political repression and psychological violence.

Ultimately they failed, and we won. Something mystical happened in the media whirlwind of May 2017, and the parade itself. It was poetic justice that Oscar López Rivera's contingent was at the head of the parade. His float was a ship, which I imagined to be a pirate ship, created by La Marqueta Retoña. It safely carried Oscar and those closest to him across a sea of Boricua pride on Fifth Avenue with Puerto Rican flags flying high and shouts of "Viva Puerto Rico!"

I do not want to romanticize. I did witness a few haters along the parade route. Yet, I saw so much power and for the first time in the parade's history, to my knowledge, a Chicago non-profit organization, "Yet She Rise", dedicated a float to the cause of ending human trafficking. Jaslene Gonzalez, born in Puerto Rico and raised in Humboldt Park, Chicago, former star of America's Top Model, graced the float decorated with a banner that read, "Save Our Culture, Save Our Girls" #saveourgirls, which made me think of the intersectionality of our struggles as a subjugated people coming full circle and moving forward.

There was sadness too. On the same day as the parade, a plebiscite, described as toothless by many activists, was scheduled in Puerto Rico. Like all past plebiscites, it changed nothing. Our island is facing a severe economic and humanitarian crisis while the U.S. government and big corporations heave austerity measures on our future.

The 2017 National Puerto Rican Day parade was a historical vindication. It lives in our collective memory as the year we officially de-corporatized and reclaimed our parade, and brought it back to its

---

wounded. The activists denounced the police and their brute force against parade goers. It was the YLP's first public defeat, and Central Committee members later admitted that they had insufficiently organized the community to understand and support this action. This history is recounted in the book, *Through the Eyes of Rebel Women: The Young Lords (1969-1976)*.

roots, celebrating our identity, our culture, and our right to be free. We will not be stopped. The people stood firm. We showed, once again, that our culture is one of our most powerful weapons. We do not need the corporations, organizations, or politicians who pulled out of the parade, or the institutions and individuals who were complicit with their silence as they cowardly hid behind a veil of neutrality. They do not represent our culture of resistance.

Those who curate knowledge, who influence how people think and shape opinions, may have a lot of power. We have power too. What is within our control is our ability to be united, to think critically and creatively. It is crucial that we tell our own stories and our narratives. We too, have the ability to curate knowledge, document our recollections and history. The 60th Anniversary of the Puerto Rican Day Parade was a transformative event. I hope that this sets a new trend and that future parades are led by the youth, by a people's color guard and a people's marching band.

I proudly marched with *35 Mujeres* in Oscar López Rivera's contingent because I love my people; I love myself, and I believe in freedom. As always, marching made me feel alive, connected to my people and myself. I want to be a part of the human story that freedom is possible—the story of freedom; a very specific freedom; the freedom of Puerto Rico and Puerto Ricans and all people fighting for their liberation.

But pride in oneself is not where it ends. It is where it begins. How do we continue to raise consciousness and build power? And how to do we continue to fight internalized colonialism, political repression and intersectional battles? These are questions better answered in action. We need to keep on marching and using our culture as strategy, tool, and weapon.

Pa'lante.

(2017)

Titi Elsie, Hurricane Maria, & Interconnected Independence for Puerto Rico

STEPHANIE LLANES

"My tia abuela is stuck in a nursing home in Hato Rey and needs to be transferred to a hospital immediately. Her sugar levels are through the roof. The roads are currently shut down but if anyone gets information about possible transportation in Hato Rey please comment below ASAP!"

My Facebook status on September 21, 2017,
a day after Hurricane Maria plummeted Puerto Rico.

I remember sitting, crying, with my eyes glued on my phone, watching images of the hurricane ravage the island for hours. At the time, my tia abuela, Titi Elsie, had been living in a nursing home for a few years. When Titi Elsie's caretaker, by some miracle, had a brief moment of cell phone signal, she called my abuela who lives in Georgia. She informed her that Titi Elsie was in critical condition due to a spike in blood sugar levels and needed to be sent to a hospital immediately. Abuela called everyone in our family in Puerto Rico for help, but there was no telephone connection to anyone. She called hospitals around the nursing home, but they all said there were no ambulance services at that time. My abuela then informed family living in the states what was happening, and we resorted to posting on social media to see if anyone could help take Titi to a hospital. Four days after the Facebook post, an ambulance finally picked her up and took her to a hospital.

Since Hurricane Maria, the political status of Puerto Rico has been a frequent topic of interest. In this reflection, I conclude that independence from the U.S. alone is not enough. I posit that to transform the crisis in which we find ourselves, we need to envision and organize toward an independent *and* interconnected Puerto Rico.

Titi Elsie's experience reflects the story of many people in Puerto Rico after Hurricane Maria (and, for some, after Hurricane Irma which struck the island on September 6, 2017 leaving more than half of Puerto Rico without power). For days and weeks, people could not reach family members, get to a hospital, access clean water or food, turn on a light, get medication, and more. Even as I write this piece, 100 days after Hurricane Maria hit, hundreds of thousands of people remain without power, over a quarter of a million people have been forced to leave Puerto Rico, and the U.S. government passed a tax bill that slams islanders—many still living without power—with a steep tax increase.

The U.S. government's response in the aftermath of Hurricane Maria was cruel, perverse, and immoral. From Donald Trump throwing paper towels at people as if at a basketball game, to tons of pounds of donations being purposefully kept at shipping docks for weeks without explanations, to Congress passing a "relief bill" that provided grants to Texas and Florida but a *loan* to Puerto Rico. For many, it was the first time they realized just how disposable Puerto Ricans are to the U.S. government. For others, such as Black folks who survived Hurricane Katrina, it wasn't a surprise but rather an all-too-familiar reminder of what happens to Black and Brown folks in this country.

Hurricane Maria is typically discussed in the context of a "natural disaster," but this narrow framing grossly ignores the realities of how the multi-pronged crisis came about and harms Puerto Ricans—those living on the island and throughout the world. Long before Hurricane Maria, reminders of colonial and corporate exploitation and neglect were all around—rampant unemployment, grossly insufficient social aid and healthcare, and home foreclosures. Eighty-four percent of Puerto Rican children were living in extreme poverty, and more than 100 public schools had closed. Moreover, President Obama had signed a bill on June 30, 2016 referred to as "PROMESA," which implemented a colonial-style fiscal board of seven non-elected U.S. officials put in charge to control and govern the Puerto Rican people. PROMESA proponents argued that their policies would address the island's "economic crisis."

In short, Hurricane Maria was not the first disaster to hit Puerto Rico; much of the destruction and suffering could have been mitigated had the U.S. government not neglected Puerto Rico's public infrastructures since 1898 (the year the U.S. murdered its way to the top of the island's colonial hierarchy). Hurricane Maria wasn't the only reason Titi Elsie wasn't at a nursing home with proper medication or why she couldn't get to a hospital sooner.

Despite Puerto Rico's current and historic challenges, we must maximize opportunities when they arise. In her book, *Emergent Strategy*, Adrianne Maree Brown explains that understanding every crisis as an opportunity "requires great emotional fortitude in practice, [and] the maturity to understand that the negative realization of that theory" can lead to an even greater disaster. With not just opportunity on our minds, but also our ancestors, seemingly more Puerto Ricans are recognizing that what is needed is ground-up, people-led organizing that shifts power. Even those who, prior to the hurricane, would've cut out their tongues before uttering a negative word about the U.S. government are wondering, "What prevents the United States from acting in exactly the same way if another category 5 hurricane plummets Puerto Rico in 2018?"

Hurricane Maria has provided an opportunity to better frame ongoing discourses about our colonial status and to support those already organizing to shift power.

What I have noticed is that discussions about Puerto Rican independence or self-determination often center on a form of nationalism that doesn't capture the transformative change many of us seek and need. Independence from the United States alone is not what will lead us to a more just, loving, and sustainable way of living. To this point, in the book *Jackson Rising,*" the authors Kali Akuno and Ajamu Nangwaya argue that "self-determination expressed as national sovereignty is a trap if the nation-state does not dislodge itself from the capitalist system. Remaining within the capitalist world-system means yielding to the domination and rule of capital, which empowers the national bourgeoisie against the rest of the population." If we apply this lesson to Puerto Rico, then we must envision a "free Puerto Rico" that includes a different economic system. If we don't, there's a good chance that elite Puerto Ricans will replicate oppressive pro-corporate, pro-war, anti-poor systems—an outcome that would leave the vast majority of Puerto Rican lives materially the same. Moreover, general rhetoric around nationalism, at times moves from a political stance of pro-independence for Puerto Rico towards one that (explicitly or implicitly) argues Puerto Rico and Puerto Ricans are superior to other countries and people. Unchecked, this nationalism becomes problematic as it essentially argues that we can be both free and separate from other people. I, as others before me, have grown to reject that worldview. A nationalistic rhetoric, without more, is partly at the root of hierarchical and oppressive ideologies, especially those used to justify white supremacy and imperialism itself.

I desire a Puerto Rico that is independent from U.S. colonialism but also that understands—and reflects in our own, future governing and economic structures—that we are connected to each other and to the earth. An interconnected independent Puerto Rico dismantles anti-Black, racist, sexist, and homophobic hierarchies of oppression—and is committed to caring for our island, the earth, and each other in a way that crosses real or constructed political, social, racial, demographic, and geographical boundaries. In short, a free Puerto Rico is one in which we all belong.

Ironically, the aftermath of Hurricane Maria gave us a glimpse of an interconnected independent Puerto Rico. The people relied on each other to survive with a sense of dignity and humanity. They cleaned up streets, shared solar energy, cooked meals for the community, rebuilt houses, shared water, and loved each other. Boricuas from the diaspora and others also mobilized support in various ways. These observations don't diminish the fact that more than one thousand people have lost their lives due to the hurricane or that people continue to face unimaginable hardships. Rather, it highlights that we are at our best when we work together from a place of love and connectedness.

This piece is a collection of thoughts and observations that I'm still developing. Writing this reflection has also been a way to deal with the sadness and feeling of impotency that resulted from witnessing what happened to nuestra isla and our people. Particularly, I offer it for those of us trying to change the humanitarian crisis facing the island.

Titi Elsie passed away on December 8, 2017. She never recuperated from the days she spent stuck at the nursing home without access to medical treatment. I wish she could have seen the support people showed her in the comments on my Facebook post—people I have never met—sharing the post, asking others for help, offering to risk their safety and drive her to a hospital. In the horrific aftermath of Hurricane Maria, the people of Puerto Rico showed us what love looks likes, that a different existence is possible, and that our survival depends on having the courage to work together towards a free and interconnected Puerto Rico.

(2017)

Urban Nature

MYRNA NIEVES

Where are my birds? They all fly high and low over the buildings, trees, rocks, and rivers of the land
Mostly seagulls and pigeons, no parrots, an occasional falcon, the rare gift of an eagle…
The clouds, gentle galloping horses, offer imaginative surprises: a giant, an otherworldly scenery, a sleeping baby resting on cotton blankets
Then there is the soothing rain that washes our spirits and nurtures the soil
Below the butterflies, worms, squirrels, and busy ants populate the ground
Sometimes lightning, earthquakes and wind bring, like the Taíno god, Huracán,
Change that renews our world and expedites karma for all
I look at my feet in the grass
Content with life on this wounded planet of my love
Sitting next to the meer with its turtles and ducks
In solace and quiet meditation
I go inside, to the inner forest where there are no polluted seas, national debts,
Wars, hungry children
Or colonization of Caribbean islands under the sun
I open my arms and deeply breathing,
I am grateful for the warmth of this early spring
A single moment on this rocky road home
I lift my face and humbly welcome
The green kiss of the Earth

This poem was written for the cultural and social project
Seven Women in Movement: www.7mujeresenmovimiento.com, 2017

An Afro-Dominicana Raised in the Bronx Supports a Free Palestine! Here's Why.

JOHANNA FERNÁNDEZ, PH.D.

In March 2016, I travelled with a U.S. delegation to Palestine to bare witness to Israel's settler colonial project in those lands and stand in solidarity with an indigenous people's struggles for survival. Like many others who have traveled internationally to advance the cause of justice, we went to uphold one of humanity's highest principles and aspirations —the notion that we should care for the freedom of others, be willing to stand with them, and bring home their voices and messages.

Our 19-member delegation included three former U.S.-held political prisoners, two former Black Panthers, trade unionists, university professors, and a younger generation of prison abolitionists and organizers. The trip was planned and led by Dr. Rabab Abdulhadi, indefatigable author and professor at San Francisco State University, who identified prisons, labor, and academic freedom as the delegation's focal points.

We met with teachers and labor organizers whose recent strikes highlighted the savage economic disparities between Palestinians and Israelis; we learned about efforts of activists and scholars to reclaim the history, political identity, and culture of the Palestinian people. The injustices we witnessed—of ongoing Palestinian displacement and demolition of homes, of attempts at dehumanizing the Palestinian people through educational policies designed to erase their culture and history, of mass incarceration and political imprisonment, and of the tragic and farcical deployment by Israelis of Holocaust-like instruments of control against Palestinians—shocked the conscience.

Although the suffering imposed on Palestinians is concentrated and acute, we were struck by structures of Palestinian oppression that resemble both contemporary and historical structures of oppression in the United States. Israel and the United States share origin histories. Both are colonial settler apartheid states. Israelis replicated in Palestine, strategies deployed by European colonialists in North America against Native Americans and other oppressed peoples.

LAND AND LABOR

Our hosts sought to illuminate root causes. They rejected narrow frameworks in international public discourse that link the contemporary crisis in Palestine to the Six-Day War of 1967 and the ongoing Israeli military occupation of the West Bank and Gaza that followed. The decisive chapter, they argued, dates back to 1948, when a Zionist military invasion usurped the vast expanse of Palestinian lands upon which the state of Israel was erected that year, consummating the Zionist, settler colonial project envisioned much earlier.

The 1948 invasion displaced 85% of Palestinians from their lands to the West Bank, Gaza and nearby Arab countries of Jordan, Syria, and Lebanon. Palestinians call this event the Nakba or "catastrophe."

The land confiscations began in 1948 continue today. Israel's Nature and Parks Authority routinely confiscates lands tilled by Palestinians with the pretext that they are "required for public purposes." The practice is straight out of the U.S. handbook, wherein sacred Indian lands were turned into national parks, from Yellowstone Park to Mount Rushmore, for "landscape preservation." And as in the case of the Bureau of Indian Affairs, established by the U.S. government in the 19th century to contain Native American communities, Israel has established a similar bureaucracy to manage matters pertaining to Bedouin Arab life.

Back in the village of Um El Heran, a modern rendition of the Homestead Act was underway. On a nearby mountain we saw a menacing bulldozer with the Israeli flag planted next to it. Like many others, this Bedouin village has been erased from Israel's map, and is therefore subject to demolition to make room for impressive European style condominiums with shopping malls and luxuries of all kinds to house the continuous flow of Zionist settlers from Europe. Upon our return to the United States, we read news reports that Um El Heran was demolished by the very bulldozers we photographed.

Other patterns of land displacement in Palestine mirror the mass acquisition of prime real estate by developers in poor, urban African American and Latino neighborhoods in the United States. Gentrification is well under way in neighborhoods with high concentrations of poor Palestinians, like Jaffa, one of the oldest ports cities in the world. The emerging architecture and aesthetic there bare a striking resemblance to gentrified Harlem, Brooklyn, the South

Bronx, and Oakland—a clear sign that real estate development is globally coordinated and designed.

In the United States, the wholesale displacement of indigenous people was accompanied by mass enslavement of Africans and acquisition of other territories during the Spanish American War of 1898, among them Puerto Rico. This shared history is the basis of solidarity between the Palestinian people and internally colonized people in the U.S.—Native Americans, African Americans, Puerto Ricans, Mexicans and Mexican Americans, Filipinos, Chinese and other people of Asian descent.

In both countries, the land grabs that accompanied the settler colonial project paved the way for industrial capitalism. A notable difference exists in the development of Israeli capitalism and its multiracial working class, however. The Israeli state has historically sought to isolate Palestinian workers from its economy and contain its reliance on this sector. In this sense the Palestinian experience is most like that of Native Americans, who suffered genocide through sporadic military raids and wars deployed preemptively by a stronger military power; as well as state engineered containment, isolation and economic strangulation in Indian reservations beginning in the 19th century.

CULTURE

School textbooks are ground zero for Israel's campaign of cultural and historical erasure. Israel has systematically eliminated references to "Palestinians" from school texts, who are now referred to as Arabs or "other people." Parallels are found in U.S. history through the Bureau of Indian Affairs, which shuttled Indian children into boarding schools and compelled them to relinquish their Indian names, culture, and language. In Puerto Rico, colonized by the United States in 1898, English was imposed as the official language in the courts and schools.

When we arrived in Palestine, Israel had just ordered the Palestinian National Authority, its indigenous surrogate agent in the occupied territories, to make illegal the playing of Palestinian music in Jerusalem's taxicabs. During our visits to cultural centers we were also told that musicians and artists who release songs with references to Palestine's history are subject to imprisonment, which has led young Palestinian artists to release their tracks anonymously on the Internet.

While Israel routinely issues notices to shut down theater, dance and music performances that challenge its colonial rule, Palestinians persist in their determination to assert their humanity through cultural expression. The murals we saw in the Ibdaa Arts Center in the Dheisheh Refugee Camp, at the Popular Arts Center in El Bireh and everywhere in Palestine stand as visually stunning challenges to the ban on resistance art on public walls imposed by the Israeli occupation.

RACIALIZED DEHUMANIZATION

European colonists in the Americas developed the architecture of racism and white supremacy. The deliberate racialized dehumanization of the people they subjugated justified their land grabs and barbaric oppression. The structure, logic, and ideology of racial oppression we witnessed in Palestine mirrored that found in the United States.

Palestinians are perceived in ways similar to African Americans: they can't work, and are unruly, "violent animals" "who live on dole." In their interactions with Palestinians at checkpoints, in the streets, and in courtrooms we visited, we witnessed the disdain, hatred, and cruelty of very young Israeli soldiers. They enforce the barbaric rules of the occupation with smug self-righteousness. As in the case of police "stops and frisk" in New York, these daily interactions with the armed foot soldiers aim to crush the dignity of the subjugated. This terror is exacerbated by the complex structures of economic and spatial isolation created in refugee camps, the siege and blockade of Gaza, and the restriction of movement and caging of communities behind the 280-mile apartheid wall in the West Bank.

Those who dare assert their humanity or interact with armed authorities pay with their lives. Between October 2015 and March 2016 alone, approximately 200 Palestinians, including 41 children, suffered summary execution in the streets at the hands of Israeli soldiers. These extra-judicial killings are justified under the guise of "safety and security," the same language U.S. police officers use to justify the killings of young Black, Latino, Asian, and Native American men, women, and children. Since the terror attacks of September 11, 2011, at least 300 sheriffs and police officers in police departments across the country, from New York and Maine and Oakland to Chicago, have traveled to Israel to receive militarized and counter-terrorism training in the methods of brutal repression mastered by the Israeli Defense Forces, which label every Palestinian a threat to Israeli security.

Israel touts itself as a nation of laws and the United States as the land of the free, yet the alarming rates at which they incarcerate their internally colonized populations make them the prison house of nations. Our delegation witnessed in plain sight the mass deployment of incarceration as a contemporary tool of colonial repression.

Palestinians face the highest incarceration rates in the world. One in five Palestinians has been imprisoned at some point in their lives by Israeli authorities. Similarly, the United States, with less than 5% of the world's inhabitants, has 25% of the world's prisoners, a disproportionate percentage of whom are the descendants of slaves. And since 1967, Israel has arrested, jailed, and tortured 800,000 Palestinian political prisoners. For its part, the United States is still holding dozens of political prisoners who were given draconian sentences for political activism during the 1960s and 1970s.

Palestinians detained in the occupied West Bank are tried and sentenced in Israeli military courts where proceedings are conducted in Hebrew, and 99% of those tried are convicted. Many are convicted with statements extracted by torture, a routine practice legalized by the Israeli Supreme Court in 1987 as "moderate physical pressure." As in the cases of Black detainees in the United States whose testimonies revealed how Chicago police coerced confessions of the innocent through torture between 1972-1991, the Palestinian prisoners with whom we met shared harrowing accounts of Israeli torture tactics.

Israel's use of incarceration and torture as tools of repression is instructive for those seeking carceral reform in the United States. Prisons are mechanisms of state repression intended to control people at the bottom of society and those most likely to resist. But in the U.S., a well-coordinated campaign of law and order ideology by the ruling class for over a half-century has obscured the underlying objectives of incarceration and consolidated public support for locking people up.

The exponential expansion in U.S. incarceration following the civil rights era was the state's attempt to restore social control—a process, which customarily follows on the heels of social uprisings. In this instance, however, the decline of the movements of the '60s, gave way to a more extreme conservative backlash. In context of the deepening crisis of urban de-industrialization, the state moved to massively incarcerate poor African American and Latino communities

—now deemed economically dispensable—for fear of their possible resistance.

CONCLUSION

Despite Israel's well-funded and heavily militarized project of repression, the Palestinian people are resilient. Yet, the daily oppression that Israel inflicts on Palestinians was, for those in our delegation, a sobering reminder of the work we must do back home to weaken, from the inside, U.S. imperialism and its support for Israel. The terrorism that the state of Israel deploys against Palestinians would not be possible without the approximately $5 billion it receives annually in U.S. military, ad hoc and special aid.

Because we witnessed structures of oppression in the Palestinian context that resembled those at home, we came closer to grasping the revolutionary principle that a victory for one is a victory for all. If the Palestinians win, we will win. This tradition of solidarity with Palestine and others around the world has a long history among oppressed persons in the United States. The young Black people who changed American society in the 1960s did not stand silent in the aftermath of the Six Day War of 1967. A SNCC statement in support for the Palestinian people read, "[W]hat happened in that war not only affects the lives of our brothers in the middle east, Africa, and Asia but also pertains to our struggle here among Black people in America."

In a world fractured by racism and xenophobia and systemic state violence, the practice of solidarity promises to enlarge our global vision, foster communal values and restore our humanity. Standing in solidarity with others and seeing others stand up against our suffering taps into our desires to fight for things greater than ourselves. But solidarity is also driven by a high level of social analysis, a deep understanding of history, and a clear grasp of the economic and political structures of subjugation across borders, which produce shared interests among the exploited and oppressed.

Today, a new generation is making these global connections and infusing new life into this tradition, from Native Americans fighting to save their water source at Standing Rock and the Movement for Black Lives to those who held their ground at Tahrir Square and those fighting austerity in Rio. In these troubled time, we have the world and a free Palestine to win.

Letter to the Revolution

NATASHA LYCIA ORA BANNAN

January 2017

Mi Querida Gente,

Antes que nada, I want you to know that you are not alone. I know your fear is real. I have received your calls ever since the election, and seen your faces as you hold your families closer. I have heard your frantic requests for information, assurance, advice, and safety. I want you to know that I see you, we—your community—sees you, and you are not alone. You will not be left alone as you wonder about the safety of your families as they walk out the door of their homes, or whether ICE will show up at your job, or if your parents who raised you here will be deported, or how to prepare your children to respond to the racial slurs and defend themselves against hate-driven violence by their classmates. As always, we will face whatever we need to together, as we have always done. *Tu no estas solo/a, el pueblo esta contigo.*

We are at a historical, and in many ways terrifying, juncture politically, where many of us feel under siege and attacked by our own government. But state violence and the targeting of our communities comes as no surprise, as our governments have done that to us throughout history. Whether it's a local anti-immigrant ordinance trying to prevent families from accessing the human right to housing, a state law prohibiting immigrants from securing drivers' licenses or making college inaccessible and unaffordable, or a court decision that permits immigration officers to lie and misrepresent themselves in order to get inside your house, our government has made survival nearly impossible for a community that is often scapegoated, shamed and exploited and has criminalized their efforts to simply live.

And yet, we will outlive Trump and his fascist-nationalist, racist and misogynist policies. Fear can only govern the oppressed or ignorant (willfully or not) for so long before people rise up in defense of themselves and the dignity of all. We have seen this throughout history, and have the examples of our brave DREAMERs and #BlackLivesMatter movement. Our existence is a threat to those who have wielded power in violent ways for too long, and it is our existence that they are attempting to eliminate. And yet, we will not be moved. We will not be forced into shadows forced to hide behind uncertain immigration status, or where we pretend the unsafe labor conditions and workplace exploitation we face are invisible to all around us. We will not go quietly into your jails and detention centers where our lives and those of our families fade into the abysmal hole of an (in)justice system where private corporations make profits off of our tortured and abused bodies. We will not be silent as you finance military might and repressive regimes in the so-cold "war on drugs" that devastates our communities and creates the horrific conditions that forces us to flee from our homes and communities. We will not allow our sisters, daughters and mothers to face cuts to essential reproductive health care services leaving them vulnerable and without options for accessing critical and affordable healthcare.

This administration underestimates us, and who we are. They clearly don't know that we organized not just historic strikes and rallies, but also fundraisers and PACs and voter registration drives, that we speak the language of an inevitable progress that cannot be detained. And when we are attacked, we all rise up. We will resist in ways we may not have had to yet, but we will resist. We will create sanctuary spaces in every community. We will educate ourselves on our rights, and we will not be afraid when your agents show up at our homes or jobs. We will not cooperate with government repression and targeting of our communities. We will build new alliances and strengthen existing ones. And we will fight back as though our lives depend on it.

Un abrazo eterno, y en resistencia y lucha,

(Posted at http://letterstotherevolution.com/natasha-lycia-ora-bannan, 2017)

Introduction to Mijente

MARISA FRANCO
CO-FOUNDER

Over the next few decades, a steady demographic shift will occur in the United States, the Latinx population is set to double. Alongside these shifts are predictions and assumptions that the power and influence of our community will grow as well. We do not believe that demographic change will automatically forge transformative change.

Because alongside these numbers of growth is the proliferating criminalization of our people, the lack of opportunity for a quality education, an erosion of government and democracy, the stealing of the commons, destruction of our planet and sinking of the economy. Organizing teaches us that no one is coming to save us; we transform ourselves in order to save ourselves, and each other. We believe a project of this sort is necessary now because real change requires more from us, not simply more of us.

"ORGANIZING TEACHES US THAT NO ONE IS COMING TO SAVE US; WE TRANSFORM OURSELVES IN ORDER TO SAVE OURSELVES, AND EACH OTHER."

The question is, how can this be done?

Our strategy is that it is through more connected and conscious leadership, it is through culture change and it is through relevant and concrete advocacy campaigns. Despite all the challenges we face, there is abundance in our community. There are Latinx people engaged in all facets of the progressive social movement in this country. We are strategists, media makers, cultural workers, action-takers, writers, base-builders, and theorists. But in many different aspects we are scattered. This is a significant gap we see.

When we say political home, what we mean by that is a space for connection, for respite, where we can sharpen our strategy and co-conspire in our own community and in community with others.

"THIS IS NOT A MOMENT TO STAY ON THE SIDELINES."

This is not a moment to stay on the sidelines. The challenges of our time demand action, and playing it safe down the middle is simply not enough. We took a closer look at advocacy and organizing infrastructure in the Latinx and Chicanx community, and we realized that there were significant gaps and shifts that should be addressed.

One is that for too long, our community has been conveniently portrayed as a single-issue voting bloc concerned only about immigration. To add insult to injury, we have seen a regression of immigration policy. Instead of progress, our futures are peddled and passed around as if they are pieces in a political game.

The impact has been that it locks out issues of U.S. born Latinxs and Chicanxs. This contributes to the disengagement of Latinx and Chicanx people in political organizing, particularly voter mobilization. If we don't see ourselves in a political agenda, or, if we don't believe in the content or viability of said agenda, we aren't going to move, much less mobilize. On the other side of this is the fact that this problem boxes in undocumented leaders to only have room to speak on immigration status or, at times, employment.

The reality is people are being excluded and targeted because of immigration status in all aspects of civil society. It is false logic, and it is wrong to silence undocumented people and their interests under the guise of incremental reforms and promises of 'we'll get to you next time.' We have the right to go for next time, *now*. We are more than our immigration status; we are more than a vote.

We hope to see and contribute to a redefinition of progressive and radical leadership in the Latinx and Chicanx community. We see a lot of climbing, and not enough lifting. By focusing on Latinx and Chicanx people, we do not mean to imply that representation is the primary solution.

It cannot be enough to stand before us armed only with a Spanish surname. We need leaders of our shared culture whose politic and commitment are ground for them to also be willing to take the risks. We need Latinx leaders who are not simply pro-Latino, but also pro-woman, pro-queer, pro-poor, pro-Black, pro-indigenous, pro-climate because OUR community is all of those things, and WE care about all

194

of them. We need to learn how to lead better with each other across these lines.

Finally, we see a need for organizations that move as quickly as life moves today, organizations that are built to be nimble and flexible, that adapt and experiment more than they predict and forecast. Because of that we are calling Mijente a hybrid form, a hub, a beehive, part digital and part bread and butter ground game organizing. We seek to engage people at different levels, from online, in the streets, in partnership and through collaboration.

Our focus is going to be developing and sparking social change and social change agents themselves. Mijente will grow to become a political home for multi-racial Latinx and Chicanx people, the warriors, the movers and shakers, the early adopters who then influence, engage and mobilize many more. Mijente will contribute and incubate new ideas, strategies and support to existing and emerging leaders. Birthed by community organizers, we don't separate the work of campaigns, advocacy, and organizing from any of this. Practice is what keeps us sharp.

A POLITICAL HOME PROMISES THE IDEA OF A WARM PLACE TO COME IN FROM THE COLD, A PLACE WHERE WE CAN SIT EASY AND LEAVE ANEW, READY TO KEEP STRIVING FOR SOMETHING BETTER, FOR ALL OF US.

The *how* of all of this looms large. There are programs and plans, goals and benchmarks but fundamentally it's about people, it's about us. What are *we willing to do?* Are we willing to learn more, be more in order to do more for our families, our partners, our communities? As many of us know, it's often times easier to step out, to give up when it is hard. We also know that there are ways where some of us, and, parts of all of us, are overlooked, excluded, and pushed out. A political home promises the idea of a warm place to come in from the cold, a place where we can sit easy and leave anew, ready to keep striving for something better, for all of us. We can sense possibility; the isolation we feel shows our desire for it. The time has come to build it.

(December 10, 2015)

Freedom

TAINA ASILI

What do we want?
Freedom!
When do we want it?
Now!

Prisons are our freedom thieves
decimate communities
destroying our families
leaving no opportunities

Racial caste alive and well
now we're called a criminal
and we're seen disposable
millions stuck in America's hell

Cannot eat the myths they've fed
high tech cages trillions spent
say no money for children
schools the pipeline to prison

Discriminate legally
employment, to vote, housing,
permanently locks the key
stealing our humanity

Chorus:

But we will evoke the lightning to strike injustice down
We will bring the thunder to break our family out
We will bring the lightning to strike injustice down
We will bring the thunder to break our family out

Freedom!

What do we want?
Freedom!
When do we want it?
Now!

ACKNOWLEDGEMENTS

Latinas: Struggles & Protests in 21st Century USA is by its very nature a collaborative project. It brings together the works of Latinas from across the country to reflect on contemporary political, economic, and cultural issues, and to document the important role that women play in bringing about social change. I am thankful for the loving enthusiasm and support that I received from so many persons to make this book a reality.

I take this opportunity to thank Deborah Paredez, my dear friend and early supporter of the project, who made possible the collaboration with CantoMundo connecting dozens of Latina poets to the anthology. I am also grateful to her for writing the Foreword, which so clearly sets the stage for the readers.

An impressive list of writers and activists submitted their work eager to be part of this collective statement and reflection. My sincerest thanks go to Amanda Alcantara, Gloria Amescua, Nia Andino, Tania Asili, Natasha Lycia Ora Bannan, Rosebud Ben-Oni, Ariana Brown, Rosa Clemente, Karla Cordero, Johanna Fernández, Maria Teresa "Mariposa" Fernández, Marisa Franco, Katherine Garcia, Claudia Sofia Garriga López, Magdalena Gómez, Jessica González-Rojas, Ysabel Y. González, Nancy Lorenza Green, Elena Gutiérrez, Jennicet Gutiérrez, Leticia Hernández-Linares, Karen Jaime, Aurora Levins Morales, Stephanie Llanes, Jennifer Maritza McCauley, Florencia Milito, Lenina Nadal, Myrna Nieves, Emily Perez, Mónica Ramírez, Raquel Reichard Carmen Rivera, Peggy Robles-Alvarado, Dominque Salas, Aida Salazar, Ruth Irupé Sanabria, Norma Liliana Valdez, Liliana Valenzuela, Vickie Vértiz, and Anjela Villarreal Ratliff.

I am grateful to Mia Roman for bringing her artistic creativity to the book cover art, making it vibrant, life-affirming, and uplifting women.

A special thank you goes to my compañero José Angel Figueroa for his encouragement, reading drafts of my writings, and giving valuable feedback on the book's content and design.

CONTRIBUTORS

AMANDA ALCANTARA is writer and journalist. Alcantara is a co-founder of *La Galería Magazine* and author of the blog *Radical Latina*. She believes in healing through art, building community, and fighting for liberation. In May 2017, she obtained a master's degree from New York University. Her thesis focused on telling the story of women from the border of the Dominican Republic and Haiti. She has a BA from Rutgers University. A map of the world turned upside down hangs on her wall.

GLORIA AMESCUA is a CantoMundo fellow and Hedgebrook alumna who has been published in various anthologies, including *Bearing the Mask: Southwestern Persona Poems, Entre Guadalupe y Malinche: Tejanas in Literature and Art,* and *The Crafty Poet II.* Amescua won the Austin Poetry Society and Christina Sergeyevna Awards, received the 2016 New Voices Award Honor for her picture book manuscript in verse, *Luz Jiménez, No Ordinary Girl,* and also won Rattle's March 2017 Ekphrastic Artist's Choice Award.

NIA ANDINO is a New York City born Afro-Boricua/Caribbean American. She is a writer and visual artist who has been a featured poet at the Nuyorican Poets Café and the Queens Lit Fest. She created the cover art for *In Defense of Glitter and Rainbows* and *Mujeres, The Magic, The Movement, The Muse.* Her art has been published in *SmokeLong Quarterly,* and her writing has been published in *Moko* Magazine, *The Abuela Stories Project* and *Mujeres, The Magic, The Movement and The Muse.* You can view her work at www.andinostyles.com

TANIA ASILI is a New York-based Puerto Rican singer, songwriter, bandleader, and activist carrying on the tradition of her ancestors, fusing past and present struggles into one soulful and defiant voice. Residing in Albany, New York, Asili performs her social justice songs as a solo artist, and also with her dynamic eight-piece band, *Taína Asili y la Banda Rebelde,* bringing love, resistance, and ancestral remembrance to venues, festivals, conferences and political events across the globe.

NATASHA LYCIA ORA BANNAN is an Associate Counsel at LatinoJustice PRLDEF, focusing on working with low-wage Latina immigrant workers as part of the LAW (Latinas at Work) initiative. Bannan is President of the National Lawyers Guild, and Co-Chairs its Subcommittee on Puerto Rico. She has advocated before international and regional human rights bodies on issues including sexual violence in armed conflict, femicide, reproductive rights violations, hate crimes, as well as human rights violations in Vieques, Puerto Rico.

ROSEBUD BEN-ONI was born to a Mexican mother and Jewish father. She is a recipient of the 2014 NYFA Fellowship in Poetry, a CantoMundo Fellow, the author of *SOLECISM* (Virtual Artists Collective, 2013), and an Editorial Advisor for VIDA: Women in Literary Arts. Her poems appear in *POETRY, The American Poetry Review, Prairie Schooner,* among others. She writes weekly for The *Kenyon Review blog,* and recently joined the Creative Writing faculty at UCLA Extension. Find her at 7TrainLove.org

ARIANA BROWN is an Afromexicana poet from San Antonio, Texas with a B.A. in African Diaspora Studies and Mexican American Studies from UT Austin. She is the recipient of two Academy of American Poets Prizes, and a 2014 national collegiate poetry slam champion. She has been dubbed a "part-time curandera" and has performed across the United States. She is currently pursuing an MFA in Poetry at the University of Pittsburgh. Follow her work at www.arianabrown.com.

ROSA CLEMENTE is an Afro-Latinx political commentator, community organizer, independent journalist, and 2008 Green Party Vice-Presidential candidate. She is currently a doctoral student in the W.E.B. Dubois department of UMASS-Amherst. Throughout her scholarly career, Clemente has been a constant on-the-ground presence through the many political struggles facing Black and Latinx people in the 21st century. She is the president and founder of Know Thy Self Productions.

KARLA CORDERO is the recipient of the 2015 Loft Literary Center Spoken Word Immersion Fellowship for writers of color (Minneapolis, MN). Cordero's chapbook, *Grasshoppers Before Gods* (2016), was published by Dancing Girl Press. Her work has appeared and is forthcoming in *Tinderbox, Word Riot, Poetry International, The Acentos Review, and Toe Good Poetry,* among other publications. She is the editor of SPITJOURNAL, an online literary review for performance poetry and social justice.

DR. JOHANNA FERNÁNDEZ teaches in the History Department at Baruch College (CUNY). Her 2014 lawsuit against the New York Police Department for its failure to release surveillance records of the Young Lords led to the recovery of the famous "*Handschu* Documents"—police surveillance records of New York political activists between 1955 and 1972. Her book on the Young Lords is forthcoming. She is the editor of *Writing on the Wall, Selected Prison Writings of Mumia Abu Jamal.*

MARIA TERESA "MARIPOSA" FERNÁNDEZ is an award-winning poet, educator, performance artist, and activist. Her poetry has been featured on HBO Latino and has been published in numerous anthologies including the *Norton Anthology of Latino Literature.* She has performed throughout the United States, Puerto Rico, South Africa, and Germany. Fernández is inspired by issues concerning the Puerto Rican diaspora, Afro-Latinidad, women's issues, social justice, and healing. She believes that poetry, art, and culture create healing spaces, community, and vital connections.

MARISA FRANCO is the co-founder and Director of the Latinx activist organization, MiJente. As an organizer and movement builder, Franco has helped lead key grassroots organizing campaigns rooted in low-income and communities of color, characterized by their innovation and effectiveness. She led the #Not1More Deportation campaign and co-authored *How We Make Change is Changing,* which describes Not1More's campaign strategy and structure that activated hundreds of organizations across sectors and communities to demand a stop to deportations.

KATHERINE GARCIA is a graduate student at the University of Wisconsin-Madison in the Gender and Women's Studies Dept. She received a BA in Radio, TV, and Film from the University of Wisconsin Oshkosh. She is passionate about LGBTQIA+ rights, domestic violence advocacy, Latinx issues, and mental health awareness, as well as 80s hair metal, used bookstores, astrology, and chocolate. You can follow her on Twitter @TheLazyVegan1.

CLAUDIA SOFIA GARRIGA LÓPEZ is a visual artist whose tree people symbolize the connection between humans and the natural world. Her inversion of the human form brings out the resemblances between legs and tree limbs, long fingers and roots, torsos and trunks. Her scholarly work is grounded in LGBT activism, and Latin America and Caribbean public policy. Her doctoral dissertation, *Gender for All: The Political Economy of Transfeminism in Ecuador,* is a historiography of transgender activism. Her article, "Transfeminist Crossroads Reimagining the Ecuadorian State" was published in the Transgender Studies Quarterly Special Edition on Transfeminism.

MAGDALENA GÓMEZ is a performance poet, playwright, keynote speaker, and lifelong arts activist. She is the co-founder and artistic director of Teatro V!da in Springfield, Massachusetts. Her book, *Shameless Woman,* a memoir in poems, published by Red Sugarcane Press, and several of her plays and poems are included in college syllabi throughout the United States. Her archives are housed at the Thomas J. Dodd Research Center at the University of Connecticut at Storrs. She may be reached through her website: www.magdalenagomez.com.

JESSICA GONZÁLEZ-ROJAS is the executive director at the National Latina Institute for Reproductive Health, the only national organization that works specifically to advance reproductive health, rights, and justice for Latinas in the United States. She has been an activist and progressive leader for two decades forging connections between social justice movements, breaking down barriers, and building a strong Latina grassroots presence. González-Rojas is an Adjunct Professor at NYU's Wagner School of Public Service and the City University of New York, and teaches courses on reproductive rights, gender, and sexuality.

YSABEL Y. GONZÁLEZ, a New Jersey native, received her BA from Rutgers University, an MFA in Poetry from Drew University and works for the Poetry Program at the Geraldine R. Dodge Foundation. She is a CantoMundo Fellow and has been published in *Tinderbox Journal, Vinyl; IMANIMAN: Poets Reflect on Transformative & Transgressive Borders Through Gloria Anzaldúa's Work; Wide Shore, Waxwing Literary Journal,* and others. Read more of her work at www.ysabelgonzalez.com.

NANCY LORENZA GREEN is an Afro-Chicana lesbian poet from El Paso, Texas who published *Crucified River/Rio Crucificado,* a collection of poetry about the murder of Mexican women in Cd. Juarez. Her poetry has been included in several anthologies; she has recorded four CDs using drums, bamboo flutes, and spoken word. As a teaching and performing artist, Ms. Green uses creative writing, music, and visual art in her cultural work with older adults and children with disabilities.

ELENA GUTIÉRREZ is an Associate Professor in Gender and Women's Studies and Latin American and Latino Studies at the University of Illinois, Chicago. Her book publications include *Undivided Rights: Women of Color Organize for Reproductive Justice* with Jael Silliman, Marlene Gerber Fried, and Loretta Ross (Boston: South End Press, October 2004) and *Fertile Matters: The Politics of Mexican-Origin Women's Reproduction* (University of Texas Press, 2008). Gutiérrez curates the Reproductive Justice Virtual Library, an online research hub that connects organizers and academic scholarship.

JENNICET GUTIÉRREZ is an undocumented Trans Latina leader with FAMILIA: TQLM in the campaign #Not1More lgbtq deportation. She was born in Tuxpan, Jalisco, México. She burst onto the national scene when she interrupted former President Obama in the summer of 2015 during his White House speech in honor of Pride month, calling attention to the struggles of Trans immigrant women. She continues to organize to end the deportation, incarceration, and criminalization of immigrants and all people of color. She currently resides in Los Angeles, California.

LETICIA HERNÁNDEZ-LINARES, a poet, interdisciplinary artist, and educator, is the author of *Mucha Muchacha, Too Much Girl*, and co-editor of *The Wandering Song: Central American Writing in the United States*. Widely published, she has performed her poemsongs throughout the country and in El Salvador. She is a three-time San Francisco Arts Commission Individual Artist Grantee, and serves on the CantoMundo Organizing Committee. An eviction fighter, she lives, works, and writes in the Mission District, San Francisco. Visit her at joinleticia.com

KAREN JAIME (Ph.D., Performance Studies, NYU) is Assistant Professor of Performing and Media Arts and Latina/o Studies at Cornell University. A former host of the Friday Night Slam at the Nuyorican Poets Café, her current monograph, *The Queer Loisaida: Performance Aesthetics at the Nuyorican Poets Café*, situates the Café as a historically queer space. Her poetry is included in: *The Best of Panic! En Vivo From the East Village*, *Flicker and Spark: A Queer Anthology of Spoken Word and Poetry*, and in a special issue of *Sinister Wisdom*, "Out Latina Lesbians."

AURORA LEVINS MORALES was born in Puerto Rico to a Puerto Rican mother and Jewish father. She was raised on the island, then in Chicago, and later relocated to the San Francisco area in the mid-1970s. Her work is widely recognized among North American feminist and Puerto Rican literary traditions. She was a contributor to *This Bridge Called My Back* and in 1986 published *Getting Home Alive* in collaboration with her mother, Rosario Morales. Levins Morales is active in Middle East peace work and the disability/chronic illness liberation movement.

STEPHANIE LLANES is originally from San Juan, Puerto Rico. She is a movement lawyer, organizer, and singer currently residing in New York City. Her work focuses on government misconduct, discriminatory policing, solitary confinement, racial justice, immigration, democracy, and Puerto Rico. Llanes believes that a different existence—a society rooted in love, justice, and sustainability—is possible, and hopes to work in community towards transformative change.

JENNIFER MARITZA MCCAULEY is a writer, teacher and Ph.D. candidate in creative writing at the University of Missouri. She is presently Contest Editor at *The Missouri Review* and the recipient of an Academy of American Poets University Award, and fellowships from Kimbilio, CantoMundo, Sundress Academy of the Arts (SAFTA), and the Knight Foundation. Her cross-genre poetry collection *SCAR ON/SCAR OFF* was published by Stalking Horse Press in 2017.

FLORENCIA MILITO, born in Argentina, is a bilingual poet, essayist, and translator whose work has appeared in *ZYZZYVA, Indiana Review, Catamaran, Entremares, Digging through the Fat, Diálogo, 92nd Street Y,* and *Kenyon Review*. A reader at Litquake, Hazel, the Inkwell, Cruzando Fronteras, and the Festival Internacional de Poesía de Rosario, she is a Hedgebrook Alumna, CantoMundo Fellow, and San Francisco Grotto Fellow. She lives in San Francisco and works as a translator and teaching artist.

IRIS MORALES is a lifelong activist, author, and the founder *of Red Sugarcane Press*. Read her bio at the *About the Editor* section. For more information, go to www.irismoralesnyc.wordpress.com.

LENINA NADAL is a mom, poet, writer, media maker, and media strategist. She has led media, strategic planning, and leadership trainings in nonprofit and grassroots organizations for the past 25 years. Currently, she is on the communications squad of the national Latinx organization, MiJente, and also the strategic communications coordinator for Global Action Project. She earned an MFA in Integrated Media Arts at Hunter College and studied historical documentary filmmaking at George Washington University.

MYRNA NIEVES, born in Puerto Rico, is a founding member of Boricua College and was director of its Winter Poetry Series for 20 years. Published books: *Libreta de sueños*; *Viaje a la lluvia*; *El Caribe: paraíso y paradoja*; *Breaking Ground: Anthology of Puerto Rican Women Writers in New York 1980-2012*; *Tripartita* (coauthor) and, with artist Yarisa Colón, *Another Version of Hansel and Gretel*. Nieves serves as Bureau Chief (curator) for the magazine *And Then*. She is co-founder of the artists group 7 Mujeres en Movimiento to support Puerto Rico. Awards: PEN Club of Puerto Rico.

EMILY PEREZ is the author of *House of Sugar, House of Stone* and *Backyard Migration Route*. She earned an MFA at the University of Houston, where she served as a poetry editor for *Gulf Coast* and taught with Writers in the Schools. A CantoMundo fellow, her poems have appeared in journals including *POETRY, Diode, Bennington Review, Borderlands,* and *DIAGRAM*. She teaches English and Gender Studies in Denver, Colorado where she lives with her husband and sons.

MÓNICA RAMÍREZ has dedicated more than two decades to eradicating gender-based violence, promoting gender equity and working to achieve political parity. She is the founder of *Esperanza: The Immigrant Women's Legal Initiative* of the Southern Poverty Law Center, *The Bandana Project*, an international project, which raises awareness about workplace sexual violence against farmworker women and *Latina Impact Fund*. Ms. Ramírez is the daughter and granddaughter of migrant farmworkers, an attorney, activist, and mother.

RAQUEL REICHARD is a journalist and editor covering Latinx social justice, political and cultural issues. Formerly the politics and culture editor at Latina magazine, her work has been published in *The New York Times, the Washington Post, Teen Vogue, Cosmopolitan, Mic, Remezcla* and more. She has a bachelor's degree in journalism and political science from the University of Central Florida and a master's degree from New

York University's Gallatin School. Born in New York to Puerto Rican parents, she spent her childhood on the island and was raised in Orlando, Fla. making her a proud NuyoFloRican.

CARMEN RIVERA is an award-winning playwright. *La Gringa* won an OBIE award and celebrated 21 years at Repertorio Español in 2017. She is the co-writer of *Celia: The Life and Music of Celia Cruz*, which played Off-Broadway. Her play *Julia De Burgos: Child Of Water* has been performed in New York City, Chicago, and Puerto Rico, and was published by Red Sugarcane Press. Ms. Rivera currently teaches playwriting at The New School and is co-director of Educational Play Productions, which brings plays about social issues to young people in public schools. For more information, check out www.carmenrivera-writer.com.

PEGGY ROBLES-ALVARADO is a tenured educator, a CantoMundo fellow, Academy for Teachers and Home School Fellow, and a two time International Latino Book Award winner. She's a 2016 BCA and Spaceworks grant recipient and a 2014 BRIO award winner. She authored *Conversations With My Skin*, *Homenaje A Las Guerreras* and created *The Abuela Stories Project* and *Mujeres, The Magic, The Movement and The Muse*. Ms. Robles-Alvarado is an MFA candidate at Pratt Institute. Contact her at robleswrites.com.

DOMINIQUE SALAS is a native of El Paso, Texas, holding an MFA in poetry from New Mexico State University. She is currently a Communication Arts Ph.D student at the University of Wisconsin–Madison focusing on rhetoric, politics, and culture. Her work has recently appeared in *Huizache, Bone Bouquet, The Volta, Apogee* and is forthcoming from *Feral Feminisms*. Find her on Twitter as @soydominique.

AIDA SALAZAR is a multi-disciplinary writer, arts administrator, and home-schooling mother who uses text to explore issues of identity and social justice. Her studies and residencies include an MFA in Writing from the California Institute of the Arts, Hedgebrook Writer's Colony, and Community of Writers at Squaw Valley. She lives in Oakland, California where she is at work on a collection of essays on healing, and numerous children's novels and picture books. Her story, *By the Light of the Moon*, is the first Chicana-themed ballet in ballet history.

RUTH IRUPÉ SANABRÍA is a poet. Her first collection, *The Strange House Testifies* (Bilingual Press), won 2nd place (Poetry) in the 2010 Latino Book Awards. Her second collection received the 2014 Letras Latinas/ Red Hen Press Award and was published in 2017. Her poems have appeared in anthologies such as *Women Writing Resistance* and *US Latino Literature Today*. She holds an MFA from NYU and a B.A. in English and Puerto Rican and Hispanic Caribbean Studies from Rutgers University. She works as a high school English teacher and lives with her husband and three children in Perth Amboy, New Jersey.

NORMA LILIANA VALDEZ, hecha en México, made her way to California in her mother's pregnant belly. She is an alumna of the VONA/Voices Writing Workshop, the Writing Program at UC Berkeley Extension, and was a 2014 Hedgebrook writer-in-residence. A member of the Macondo Writers' Workshop and a CantoMundo fellow, her poems appear in *Calyx, Huizache,* and *Tinderbox Poetry Journal,* among others. A Bay Area educator, she dedicates her life's work to uplifting first-generation college students.

LILIANA VALENZUELA is the author of *Codex of Journeys: Bendito Camino* (Mouthfeel Press, 2013). Her poetry has appeared in *Edinburgh Review, Indiana Review, Tigertail, Huizache,* and other publications in Mexico, Spain, Argentina, and the United States. An inaugural fellow of CantoMundo and a long-time member of the Macondo Writers Workshop, Valenzuela has received awards and recognition from Luz Bilingual Publishing, Austin International Poetry Festival, Drunken Boat, Indiana Review, Austin Poetry Society, and the Chicano/Latino Literary Award.

VICKIE VÉRTIZ was born and raised in Southeast Los Angeles, California. A Lucille Clifton Scholar at the Community of Writers, she was also the 2016 Poetry Center Fellow at the University of Arizona, Tucson. Her second poetry collection, *Palm Frond with Its Throat Cut,* was published in 2017 by the University of Arizona Press, Camino del Sol series. A graduate of Williams College, U.T. Austin and U.C. Riverside, she teaches creative writing nationally.

ANJELA VILLARREAL RATLIFF's poems have appeared in various publications, including *Chachalaca Review, Pilgrimage; wild voices: an anthology of poetry & art by women; Lifting the Sky: Southwestern Haiku & Haiga; Cantos al Sexto Sol: An Anthology of Aztlanahuac Writing; The*

Enigmatist, Blue Hole; The Crafty Poet II: A Portable Workshop; Texas Poetry Calendar, Australian Latino Press, di-vêrsé-city; Bearing the Mask: Southwestern Persona Poems; Boundless, The Cherita: Your Storybook Journal, and forthcoming in *RiverSedge*. A native Tejana, she was raised in southern California and has resided in Austin, Texas since 1990.

About CantoMundo

In the summer of 2009, Deborah Paredez joined fellow Tejana/o poets, Norma E. Cantú, Celeste Mendoza, Pablo Miguel Martínez, and Carmen Tafolla around Norma's kitchen table and dreamed of a world where Latina/o poets could regularly gather in a community of creative inspiration and mutual support. They dreamed of and then set about building a "song-world," a canto-mundo, and by the next summer they were hosting their first writing retreat for Latina/o poets.

CantoMundo is a national organization that cultivates a community of Latina/o poets through workshops, symposia, and public readings. Founded in 2009, CantoMundo hosts an annual poetry workshop for Latina/o poets that provides a space for the creation, documentation, and critical analysis of Latina/o poetry.

Inspired by Cave Canem and Kundiman (organizations for African American and Asian American poets), CantoMundo issues a national call for applications every year and selects new fellows who, once accepted, are eligible to return to the annual writing retreat up to three times, thereby fostering long-term support and collaborations. They join returning fellows who are fulfilling their three-year commitment and who provide mentorship and guidance to the incoming fellows.

CantoMundo's first gathering convened in 2010 at the National Hispanic Cultural Center in Albuquerque, New Mexico. From 2011-2016, the workshops were held at the University of Texas at Austin. CantoMundo has received support from the National Endowment for the Arts, the Academy of American Poets, the University of Texas's Center for Mexican American Studies, and Columbia University's Division of Arts and Sciences. CantoMundo is currently based at Columbia University in New York City.

www.cantomundo.org

ABOUT THE BOOK COVER ARTIST

Mia Roman is a seasoned traveler and self-taught fourth-generation artist with a business degree, a passion for art, and certified as a Medicine Woman in energetic holistic indigenous bodywork. An internationally recognized visual and mixed media artist, curator, expressive arts facilitator, advocate, educator and entrepreneur, Roman's visual works have appeared in numerous exhibitions, universities, galleries and reside in many private collections. Her paintings reflect spirituality, culture, humanism, reality, and advocate for women.

Roman is on a mission to supply tools and space where people can explore, heal, and discover themselves freely through creative play. She founded The Women's Temple where art is healing, and nature is medicine to wholeness while learning and preserving Indigenous culture and tradition. She has curated shows such as *Visions of Puerto Rico, Latinas En Foco, Women's Journey, FEMICIDE,* and *FAREWELL SILENCE,* which was a global collaboration of more than 300 women sharing their voices through visual arts, and pen and paper.

A passionate educator, Roman has taught at the Children's Art Carnival, Riverbank New York State Park, The Leroy Neiman Arts Center, The Westbeth Arts Center, La Casa Azul Bookstore, and the Clemente Soto Velez Cultural and Educational Center. She co-founded and facilitated an Expressive Arts program for homeless and displaced children and families at the Ruth Fernandez Family Residence in the South Bronx. She also conducts private group art/creative workshops, medicine drum and rattle making classes, and Shamanic healing circles.

www.artsbymia.org

About the Editor

Iris Morales is the founder and executive editor of Red Sugarcane Press; she is a lifelong activist and educator dedicated to human rights and the decolonization of Puerto Rico. Her community activism, and love of history and storytelling, led her to media production, publishing, and writing.

Morales is the author of *Through the Eyes of Rebel Women, The Young Lords, 1969 to 1976;* this first account of women's experiences in the organization was published in 2016. Her award-winning documentary, *¡Palante, Siempre Palante!, The Young Lords* premiered on national public television in 1996 and continues to introduce audiences to the social justice movements of Puerto Ricans in the United States during the 1960s and 1970s. Morales was a leading member of the Young Lords Party, co-founder of its affiliated Women's Union, and co-leader of the Philadelphia chapter of the Puerto Rican Revolutionary Workers Organization. Her writings about this period have been widely anthologized and appear in *The Norton Anthology of Latino Literature, PALANTE: Voices and Photographs of the Young Lords, 1969-1971,* and in dozens of college readers.

A native New Yorker, Morales holds a JD from the New York University School of Law where she was a Root-Tilden Scholar. She subsequently earned an MFA in Integrated Media Arts at Hunter College.

Morales is the recipient of numerous awards, including the Global Citizen Award from the International Youth Leadership Institute, Latin Roots East Harlem Living History Award, the Bayard Rustin Award for Social Justice, and the Special Recognition Award from the International Latino Film Festival, among many others.

About Red Sugarcane Press, Inc.

Red Sugarcane Press, Inc. was formed in 2012 as an independent publisher to present the history and culture of the Puerto Rican, Latinx, and African Diasporas in the Americas. The distinct voices and artistic styles of its authors deepen and broaden our knowledge about history and contemporary social, political, and cultural issues. They introduce forgotten or unknown stories from the journey of Indigenous and African people in the Americas who from enslavement to the present have triumphed through the courage and tenacity of many generations.

Red Sugarcane Press seeks to inspire the exchange of ideas and encourage participation in the struggle for human liberation.

www.RedSugarcanePress.com
facebook.com/redsugarcanepress